Books by Joy Collins

Second Chance 2007
Coming Together (with Joyce Norman) 2009
I Will Never Leave You 2017

I Will Never Leave You

Joy Collins

Desert Spirit Press

Arizona

Copyright © 2017 Joy Collins

Author's Note

Desert Spirit Press, LLC
www.DesertSpiritPress.com
DesertSpiritPress@cox.net

ISBN:
978-0-9889850-3-2

Printed in the United States of America
First Edition

Author photo: Photography by Leanna http://photosbyleanna.com/

To John
For always believing in me
For always loving me
Still

Acknowledgments
CB

Where to start? There are so many people whom I need to acknowledge and thank for their part in helping this book come to be.

To Susanne Wilson for introducing me to my "team" on the Other Side. She and they kept encouraging me to keep on writing when the task seemed so hard. And a big Thank You for honoring me with this beautiful Foreword.

To my soul sisters Cathy Marley and Betts McCalla for always being there with hearts and shoulders.

To my family and friends who supported me after John passed and kept me strong.

To my beta readers – Joyce Norman, Shelley Uram, Claudia Flowers, and Cynthia Flowers – they helped make this book so much better.

To my fur-babies past and present. You showered me with unconditional love and gave me a reason for getting up in the morning.

And last – but never ever least – to John. You inspired and encouraged me in both life and death. You showed me a way when I was at my darkest. You loved me – and still do – and that has made all the difference in my life.

Thank you, Sweetheart.

Until we are together again..........

Foreword

CฮƆ

    I first met Joy two years after her soul mate John had unexpectedly transitioned. She was still deeply immersed in grief over the loss and driven by questions she had been unable to answer. Where was he? Was he okay? Was he to be forever beyond her reach? She had been reading one grief book after another, but nothing provided the answers she needed.

    When Joy came to me, she had seen other mediums. She knew that her husband's consciousness, all his memories and personality, were still very much alive. She wanted more than just a reading with a spiritual medium. Joy wanted to learn how to make her own, direct connection with John's spirit. Seeking understanding and connection, she began taking the next steps in her journey. I was honored when Joy chose me as a teacher on her path. She eagerly studied every course I had to offer, progressing through classes including Reiki Master Teacher, Intuition Development, and Past Life Regression. Her connection to her husband in spirit was becoming stronger, week by week. It was only a matter of time (and trust).

Joy was quick to connect with her spirit guides and become comfortable communicating with them. Soon her spirit guides were "showing" us a book (which became the book you are reading now). Joy's spirit guides used the symbols of hands and angel wings as their way of saying that the spirit world supported her in writing this book.

It was not an easy process, but grief is never easy. Joy's intense connection to John kept her moving forward on her spiritual journey. She knew that death was like a change of address and "moving away" cannot end a true love story. They now have a new relationship that is transcendent of Earthly life. All I had to do was facilitate and watch the two of them recreate the magic that they always had!

As sure as I am that the sun will rise in the morning, I am certain that Joy and John (in spirit) wrote this book together. With great compassion and generosity, this couple now shares their story, to help others heal from grief and learn to reconnect after death.

This book is about love, heartbreak, and healing in the face of the loss of one's soul mate. You will find no grief counseling and no scientific data here. Joy is not a spiritual medium; she is a regular person like you. But if you have lost the love of your life, whether a spouse, child, or other greatly loved person, I invite you to come along on this journey now. Perhaps you, too, will be inspired to create a different kind of relationship with your loved one in spirit.

Love lives forever!

Susanne Wilson
The Carefree Medium
December 2016
www.carefreemedium.com

Introduction

CB

Why am I writing yet another book about grief? Or, more specifically, why I am writing about *my* grief?

Seems rather conceited, doesn't it?

I guess I have three reasons.

- I want to explain that grief is still largely misunderstood in our society and those who are mourning are given a harder row to hoe because of expectations put on them by those who don't understand.

- I want to show that losing a soul mate spouse is very hard. In my opinion, it is harder than losing a spouse who is not your soul mate. I do not say this out of arrogance. And I'm not saying my grief is better than your grief. This isn't a contest. I am just acknowledging that not all marriages are between soul mates. And that's okay. But those of us who are married to soul mates mourn a little differently when we lose our partner. Those of you who are going through this will understand only too well. My hope is that this book will explain that.

- And finally, I want to share, through my story, that love, and life, don't end just because death happened. I confirm up front that there is a lot of my life experience in this book. And a lot about John. Some of my editing team even questioned if maybe there were too many "John stories" in here. It is deliberate. I tell these stories not only to give you a feel for the depth of what a soul mate relationship is like, but also how soul mates can continue their love even after death.

Let me elaborate.

John was truly my soul mate. And yes, that term gets thrown around a lot these days. Just because you are madly in love with someone doesn't mean he or she is your soul mate. You can have a wonderful marriage with someone who isn't your soul mate. The two aren't mutually exclusive. But when you are living your life with your soul mate, especially if that soul mate is also your Twin Flame, life is beyond wonderful. And when you lose that person to death, the depth of the devastation is almost something that can't be put into mere words. Having said that, I am going to try to do just that in this book.

Grief is hard. Grief is terrible. Grief is work. And society, especially American society, has put labels and restrictions and expectations on grief that are totally unrealistic and, in some cases, downright harmful. My first year after losing John was without a doubt the worst year of my life. I cried – all the time. I lost weight. I had no interest in life. Was I suicidal? No. Was I depressed? Yes, in the sense that I was very sad and had little to no interest in anything going on around me. Did I take care of myself and my home and my animals? Absolutely. Well, mostly what I did was for my home and my animals and doing the minimum for myself. I did not sit around on the sofa (most days) inside a mound of used tissues.

Yet, every time I went to the doctor and shed a tear, I was handed samples and prescriptions for antidepressants. I read books and articles that diagnosed me, and those suffering like me, with "complicated" grief because it went on for longer than six months. Other books stated that I should already have given away all of John's clothes and taken off my wedding ring. Everywhere I turned it seemed someone had an opinion about what I *should* be doing and how I *should* be feeling. None of them were right. ***Grief is an individual thing. We each go through it in our own way. And doing what felt right for me was not a wrong thing. In fact, it was the most right thing I could do.*** Especially given the underlying circumstance that I was grieving the loss of my soul mate/twin flame.

And finally, partly because I had the need to know and partly because I just knew in my heart of hearts that this was true, I searched for the answer to the question that haunted me the most. Was it possible to continue my relationship with John even though he had passed? From the very first day I knew that, if any couple could do it, we could. I knew how much we loved each other. I knew how much we were part of each other's lives. And I knew that we could do this.

Was it possible though? Was I just grasping for something because I was deep in grief? Or was there something to all the metaphysical stuff I had learned up until that point? Not only did I learn the answers to those questions, I learned even more than I realized was possible. Death is an illusion and communication with loved ones who have passed is not only possible but practical and happening all the time if we but know how to receive the messages.

I want to be clear about some things, too. I am not special. I'm an ordinary woman. I am not psychic. I am not a medium. Even though this is my story, this is not about me. I use my experience as an example. This book is for others who are grieving, especially those – man or woman – who are grieving their soul mate. I want to show you that any one of you can communicate with your loved one who has passed.

I also want to be clear that this is not the definitive book on grief and communication with a loved one who has passed. Just the opposite is true. This book is only the beginning. My hope is that I will whet your appetite and guide you to want to learn more.

Early on in my journey after John passed, I meditated with the expressed intention of learning my purpose. It was becoming apparent to me that if I was still here, despite my longing not to be, that maybe, just maybe, there was a reason. Maybe I still had something to do.

So, I meditated as best I could and asked for an answer. What I got was "Be. Do. Teach."

A strange answer, indeed. Assuming I wasn't tapping into my inner Yoda, what did it mean? I had no clue. Did it refer to my blossoming interest in Reiki? Maybe. But that didn't feel like it.

So, I let it go, I prayed the answer would come in time.

And eventually it did.

I realized as I started to write this book that "Be – Do – Teach" is its theme. I have divided the book into those three parts. The first part "Be" is our story – John's and mine. In it, I lay the groundwork to show you how we were together and why we still are. The second part is "Do" where I show you how I learned to apply what I was learning so that our relationship continues to this day. And the third part is "Teach". There I am going to guide you on the beginnings of your own journey to communication with your loved one.

I invite you to come along with me through the last few years of my life and see if what I have to say will resonate with you and perhaps help you along your way as well.

And so it is…

Joy
September 2016

PART ONE

BE

Our Story

Chapter One

C3

    I looked at the clock radio on the hotel nightstand – 1:15 AM – and turned to check John's side of the bed. He wasn't there. Nothing unusual. He often got up in the middle of the night to pee. One of the hazards of being a sixty-seven-year old man.

    But he hadn't been in bed when I woke up at 12:30 AM either.

    Right away this didn't feel right.

    I called John's name.

    No answer.

    I was instantly and fully awake. I didn't bother to turn on the bedside lamp. I could see a sliver of light coming from the bathroom door. As soon as I jumped out of bed I hit my shin on the arm chair next to the bed. Cursing my stupidity, I limped around the bed calling John's name again.

    Still no answer.

    I was now panicking.

Joy Collins

John and I lived in Arizona and we had been visiting my family in New York City. But the visit was over. We had walked back to our hotel holding hands the evening before and I thought life couldn't get any better. That night we had snuggled under the covers and talked about going home and how much we were looking forward to our own bed and our animals. We wished each other Good Night, I rolled over and quickly fell asleep. It was 10:30 and I knew the wake-up call would come early.

Now fear gripped me as I stumbled around the unfamiliar room.

I called John's name again. Still no answer. Not even a moan.

Time slowed down. What took mere fractions of seconds felt like forever as I made my way to the bathroom.

By now I had rounded the bed and could see the bathroom door more clearly. It was slightly ajar. As I neared the door, I saw John's right foot beyond. It was discolored, oddly bluish-purple. And there was no way his foot should have been so close to the door like that. John was a tall man but even I knew he had to be slightly stretched out to reach the door like that. Had he fallen?

"John, are you okay?"

I reached the door and pushed it open, knowing in my heart that something was terribly wrong.

The next second changed my life forever.

"John!"

My brain just exploded. This couldn't be happening.

John was sitting on the toilet, slumped toward the wall. His eyes were half closed, and the right side of his face looked drooped. His left leg was slightly drawn up, his left arm was across his chest and his right arm and leg were extended. I screamed his name again and reached for him. His body was cold and already felt slightly stiff. I shook him knowing it was useless.

"John!" I kissed him. "John."

I ran from the bathroom and just spun in place in the small room, screaming and crying.

24

After a second, I turned toward the bed and reached for the phone on the bedside table. I knew I needed help. I wasn't wearing my glasses and couldn't see to know what numbers to push to get the front desk. I just kept hitting buttons, getting nowhere, crying and sobbing. Finally, I took a deep breath and took the time to get my glasses and put them on. I now clearly saw what I needed and the man at the front desk answered immediately.

"Front desk, may I help you?"

I know I screamed at the poor man. "My husband is dead, and I need help!"

"Ma'am? I'll be right there." He disconnected.

I sat in the lone armchair in the room. This couldn't be happening. This wasn't real. I looked at the bathroom doorway again. The room was eerily quiet. I ran back in and touched John again, crying, pleading with him to come back to me.

But he was gone. I was alone. All alone. The world had turned upside down and nothing made sense.

I went back out to the room and sat in the chair, waiting for the man from the front desk.

I looked at the ceiling. Was John still here? Could he hear me?

"I love you, Baby. Please come back. I don't want to do this. Please." I sobbed as if my insides were falling out.

But there was no answer.

Nothing.

Silence.

Nothing except the sound of my own crying.

Chapter Two

CB

The day I married John was the happiest day of my life.

John and I had been living together for a little over a year when we married in August of 1981. We had met almost five years earlier in November 1976 at a day treatment and counseling center for emotionally disturbed children and adolescents in northeastern Pennsylvania. I was the new nurse at the facility and John was one of the counselor/therapists. At the time, I was married to Bill, a psychiatrist. Bill was working at the local mental health center and had heard of the job through his networking circle. So, he recommended me and I was given an interview. The job paid poorly, even for that time and area of the country, but I was just happy to be working. Bill and I had no children, just two cats and a parakeet, and I was bored out of my mind at home.

I will never forget the day I met John. I was still in orientation and was attending my first full staff meeting in the main building. John was sitting against the far wall in front of a window next to a psychologist friend. He stood out for some reason. Maybe it was the full red beard and the almost shoulder-length red hair.

Or maybe my soul just knew. John and I always believed we recognized each other from all the lives we had spent together both in this world and in between. All these years later I can still see him in my mind on that first day. It was as if a light beamed down from on high and singled him out. My heart recognized him and knew it was home. I imagine there was a metaphysical sigh of relief. "At last. There you are."

And the older we got and the longer we were married, the more we believed it. In any case, at the time, there was an instant rapport and an instant attraction that we both fought for a few years. But eventually we developed an easy friendship that soon blossomed into love.

I divorced Bill in 1978. The marriage had always been rocky and finally Bill's drinking and abuse got to be too much, and I threw in the towel. John separated from his first wife in 1980. He moved in with me and our life together began in earnest. We had our challenges but we both knew we were meant to be together.

We decided to marry in August 1981. I think we had always known we would be married someday but had never made any real plans. Then one day we were sitting in our favorite bar, talking "how about?" and "what if?" Three weeks later we were standing in front of a justice of the peace pledging to love each other forever.

Our wedding day was magical because it was our wedding day. Technically we were eloping because we had only told a few of our closest friends that we were getting married. Neither of our families knew what was happening but we had a small reception planned at that same bar where we had made our decision to get married. That deserves its own story.

This bar – actually, it was more of a fancy lounge with small cubicles and sofas placed all around - was called Vispi's and had burned down in the spring of 1981. Okay, it was kind of a gay hangout, too. The decor was over the top with red flocked wallpaper and large paintings of nudes all over, but it was a fun place, always packed with people – gay and straight – having a good time and we loved going there. John and I had gotten to know the owner and the bartenders and wait staff. We were glad to see it reopen that summer. When we told them of our wedding plans, they made us a deal. They were trying to entice business back and saw this as a way to help all of us. If we had our reception there they would give us hors d'oeuvres and open bar – including a champagne toast! – for three hours for thirty dollars. We were expecting about twenty people and this was an offer we couldn't pass up. We were only too happy to agree.

Of course, we needed a wedding cake and the bartender gave us the name of a man who baked cakes and sold them out of his home. So off we went. The man and his wife were darling and very friendly.

Turned out that he had learned to bake while in prison.

For manslaughter.

Oh, well, the cake was only ten dollars. We were grateful.

So, the happy day arrived. John, ever the careful planner, decided to call the judge's office where we were scheduled to be married to make sure all was set for that afternoon. It was a good thing he did because the judge was on vacation. It seemed our wedding was never placed on his schedule. If John hadn't called, we would never have known. It took some scrambling, but we found a judge who was available for that afternoon. He was busy but his receptionist said they could squeeze us in.

And squeeze us in they did. When we arrived at three in the afternoon, the judge was busy dealing with some young kid in the back room. I have no idea what was going on but all I saw was someone handcuffed to a desk and the judge sitting opposite him. When we and our witnesses arrived, the judge told the kid he would be back, put on his robe and a smile, and married us in the front room. Despite the odd circumstances, it was still the best day of our life.

And the reception was wonderful. Unbeknownst to me, John had ordered a balloon bouquet to be delivered to me at the reception.

It was at the time when balloon bouquets were just becoming popular. I had no idea he had set this up. So, right after we cut our cake and did the traditional feeding of each other, a woman dressed up like Little Bo Peep arrived with a dozen balloons and sang "Ain't She Sweet" to me as she handed me the bouquet. John never believed he was a romantic, but he did things like that all the time. He *was* a romantic and I loved him for it.

Later that evening we went out to dinner with our Maid of Honor and her husband. My best friend from nursing school, Judy, and her husband John, had driven up from southern Pennsylvania where they had been visiting family just so Judy could be in our wedding. They were leaving later that night and we wanted to spend some more time with them before they left. We were at the Crackerbox Palace, another favorite hangout where John and I often went to eat and dance. We wanted them to play "You Needed Me" by Anne Murray. It was "our song" and we wanted that to be our first dance as a married couple. But the deejay didn't have that song, so he played another Anne Murray song for us. I can't remember what song it was now. It might have been "Tennessee Waltz". It doesn't matter. We were married and dancing and happy and that's all we cared about.

Chapter Three

CB

Life with John was an adventure. John's attitude toward life was happy and more relaxed than mine and I learned a lot from him. With him I felt free to take chances and try things I had never done before. One of those things was camping - tent camping to be exact. I had never slept in a tent before. I had never made a campfire or roasted marshmallows. I had never used a communal bathroom or shower. But I did all that and more with John. Camping was cheap so there was that, but it was also fun. Sitting under the stars, watching the flames of our campfire, waking up to the sounds of the forest – it was the closest thing to Heaven.

Not all our adventures were stress free. I often told people that most of my married life was one continual house remodel. Our first house together was right after we were married. John was given the opportunity to buy the house he had shared with his ex as part of the divorce settlement. So, three months after we were married, we moved into the little house in Dallas, Pennsylvania. My bargaining chip was that I would do this only if John remodeled the kitchen and repainted every surface of the house. It was hard enough moving into his former house and neighborhood. I needed to make the space my own. So, John and I painted all the rooms. We put wall to wall carpeting down in the living room. And John took the kitchen down to the studs and rebuilt it, including making new cabinets from lumber complete with handmade stained-glass doors. They were truly a thing of beauty. But it took forever.

In between all of this, John went back to school. We knew that at some point in time we would probably be leaving that part of Pennsylvania, maybe even leaving the state. John had a bachelor's degree in Psychology and everything he needed to obtain his Masters degree except for his thesis. But even if he completed his Masters, therapist positions did not pay that well. In the meantime, he saw how well I was doing as a nurse (by this time I was a nurse manager at a local psychiatric hospital), so John decided to become a nurse. With all the college credits he already had, all he needed to graduate were his nursing courses. Amazingly, John worked full time and attended school full-time and in June 1985, he graduated from nursing school. By this time, he had finished remodeling the house and we decided to sell it. We knew we needed our own place. It had always been our plan to get a home that was truly just our own with no ghosts from the past. Unfortunately, the house sold very quickly (John had done an excellent job of remodeling) and we hadn't yet found a house we liked so our real estate agent helped us find a place to rent in the interim while we continued to look for our dream home.

But instead of getting rid of ghosts we found more. The house we rented was at the end of a dirt road called 42nd Street. I think that was somebody's idea of a joke. The house itself was darling. Built in the late 1700's it was small but very charming. It had a huge kitchen with a small mud room and a good size living room and bathroom (the only one) downstairs. Upstairs were two bedrooms with a single hall closet. It was obvious that the house had been built in bits and pieces over the years. Probably the best part of the house was the solarium. It ran the length of the entire downstairs and had views of the surrounding woods. We moved in in June 1985 and stayed until November that same year and watched the seasons change from those windows.

After graduation, John secured a part-time job as a night nurse at the same hospital I was working in but on a different unit. This gave him lots of time to look for our house. After many searches, he found it. He called me at my office at the hospital.

"I found the house." I could hear the happiness in his voice but there was something else too. I just couldn't put my finger on it.

"Great. Where is it?"

"Lehman." I knew where that was. It was just a few miles further out than our house in Dallas and not far from the house we were renting. We had driven around that area several times looking for houses. "I want you to take a ride out there and go look at it."

"Now?"

"Yes, if you agree, we need to make an offer. I'm really excited about this. But it needs work."

Coming from John, those could be scary words.

"What do you mean 'it needs work'?"

"Just go look at it and then call me back." I could hear a smile in his words and sensed trouble.

John gave me directions and a final warning. "Just remember to look at it with future eyes."

It was already lunchtime, so I told my staff I needed to go out for a while and headed out to this wonderful house that had John all excited.

Thirty minutes later I stood in front of a house that looked like it was out of a horror movie. It was an old two-story Victorian farmhouse that had once been white when it had seen better days. Looking at it from the front, the entire house sagged on the right side. It had a wraparound porch that was screened in. The two huge old trees in the front lawn had been dropping leaves on the house for years and it seemed every leaf had embedded itself in those screens giving the house a dark and dreary look. There was aluminum skirting under the porch, and it was either sagging or missing in some places. The grass needed mowing.

Cue the creepy organ music.

I looked down at the paper in my hand on which I had written the directions John had given me. Surely, I had made a mistake. This couldn't be the dream home he wanted. I looked around the neighborhood but there was no other house that fit his directions.

Confused, I headed back to my office. I was convinced I had not found the house and was disappointed.

As soon as I was back at my desk, I called John.

"Well, what did you think?"

"I'm sorry, hon. I must have made a mistake. I couldn't find the house."

John repeated the directions.

"Yes, that's where I went but I only saw this old dilapidated house that looked like it was falling over."

John was now laughing. "That's it."

"You're not serious. That's the house you want to buy? Are you crazy?"

"It will be beautiful. Trust me. I can do it. The house needs to be jacked up and the sill needs to be replaced but it has good potential. I can make it into a showplace." John had been inside the house already with the realtor and had obviously been remodeling the house in his head.

Somehow, I let myself get talked into buying that house. When I later got the grand tour, it was even worse on the inside. A part of the floor was missing in the kitchen. There was no central heat. The only source of heat in the house was a coal stove in the kitchen. There was a vent through the ceiling to the room above (the master bedroom) and the heat rose through that and heated the upstairs. The downstairs bathroom was a little cubby off the kitchen that was so filthy I didn't even want to walk in to look at it. There was ugly wallpaper everywhere, even on the ceilings. The water stains made spooky faces at me. There was a summer kitchen off the back of the main kitchen and that was piled high with debris. And there was no garage.

But the grounds were beautiful. It was a corner lot and very spacious. The house had been built around 1860 and obviously had some charm to it. My husband was smitten, and I succumbed to his enthusiasm. We bought the house for very little money. The house had been owned by three sisters and their respective husbands. Their father Charlie had been living in the house by himself after his wife died. He himself had died only months before. Apparently, he had raised prize-winning tomatoes in his garden in the back yard. For Christmas, the year before, he had received a new tiller as a present and he had gone out in the spring to get the soil ready for his new crop. He turned on that spiffy new high-powered tiller and promptly keeled over. He was found by a friend, dead as a doornail, tiller still running.

Getting three elderly sisters and their husbands to agree to a price wasn't easy but we did it and took possession in August 1985. John spent the next few months jacking up the house, replacing the sill, putting in central heat, making us a new halfway decent bathroom, and fixing the siding and rotten floor so we could at least move in without wind blowing through the walls.

Now for the ghost stories.

That November, our friends helped us move the big pieces of furniture and heavier boxes from the rental house on 42nd Street but John and I still had to make a few trips back and forth on our own to pack up our clothes and some other items. I went alone one Saturday afternoon to gather my clothes from our bedroom upstairs. While I was packing, I kept hearing the door from the spare bedroom down the hall knock against the wall. I thought this was strange since no windows were open, so I left my packing and went to investigate. Although I could not find a reason for the noise, I decided to reposition the door away from the door jamb anyway and went back to my work.

The door started knocking again.

A second time, I looked, repositioned the door, and went back to my packing.

35

Joy Collins

Again, I heard that same knocking, door against wall.

Okay, now I was spooked.

I quickly went downstairs, trying to decide what to do.

Now, I thought I heard very slight whispering. No words, just an undercurrent of almost white noise. That was it. I left everything where it was and drove back to the house in Lehman.

John was working in the kitchen.

"Back so soon?" John took one look at my face and knew something was wrong. "What's the matter? What happened?"

"You're not going to believe this, but I think the house is haunted. I heard things." I told him about the door knocking and the voices.

John just smiled. "You're kidding, right? The house isn't haunted. We lived there for six months. We never heard anything."

"Maybe they don't want us to leave. But I swear I heard stuff over there. I'm not going back there by myself."

"You're letting your imagination run away with you. There are no ghosts over there. Joy, you're being silly. I'm going over there."

"Fine but I'm staying here."

John and I both believed in ghosts. We had just never experienced them. So off he went in his car while I worked on unpacking in the new house. He was back within half an hour and I could tell from the look on his face that something had happened.

"I heard the whispering," he said.

"See? I told you."

"Okay, from now on we go back there together, and we pack up fast."

We both felt uncomfortable going back and were never sure if we heard actual whispering or if it was our imagination, but the door stopped knocking.

Then there was Charlie. Remember the man who died in our backyard tilling the soil?

When we moved in there was an old ratty rocking chair left by the coal stove. The upholstery was worn and frayed, and the

36

stuffing was coming out, but we didn't have the heart to throw it away. We knew it had belonged to Charlie so, out of respect, we put it up in the attic when we moved in.

That Christmas, John's children came to visit. The house had four bedrooms on the second floor. We had made up the larger front bedroom for the two girls and John's son was in one of the smaller rooms toward the back. The morning after their first night with us, we were all sitting around the breakfast table and we asked them how they had slept in their new rooms. The girls looked at each other, unsure what to say. There was something wrong.

"We didn't sleep so well. We heard noises."

"Well, this is an old house," John said. "It makes lots of creaks at night."

"This was different. It sounded like a rocking chair. It was right over our bed. It scared us."

John and I looked at each other and he made a face to me that I knew meant "keep your mouth shut." It was obvious the girls had been spooked.

"It was probably squirrels. I'll go up there and look and get rid of them."

Later that day John went up in the attic. Sure enough, there was Charlie's rocking chair right over the girls' bedroom. Could it really have been Charlie rocking away during the night just as he had so many nights next to the coal stove? John wasn't taking any chances.

"Charlie, please don't rock the chair. You're scaring the kids."

John told me what he had done. It sounded silly but a part of us really believed it was Charlie rocking the chair.

The next night all was quiet. We never heard the chair again. And that chair stayed there until we moved out several years later.

We had many other "adventures" in that house.

Like the time Meow-Meow, one of our cats, decided to go out our bedroom window via the little accordion sleeve next to the window air conditioner. She was too smart for her own good and

Joy Collins

figured out how to push it open. From there it was a simple procedure to get out onto the roof. Only thing was she didn't know how to get back in. Luckily John was walking our dog Willie outside and Willie started barking his head off and looking up at the roof. John immediately saw the problem but wasn't sure about a solution. He finally decided to hook up his longest ladder and climb up. He also nailed a box to a long wooden rod and placed an open can of cat food inside. The idea was to scoop the cat up when she went inside. In hindsight, it probably seemed better inside his head. In any case, there was John up two stories-plus alongside the house. Meow-Meow was within reach. She did head toward the box but started sliding instead. Just as she plummeted past John he reached out and grabbed her leg. He was able to save her and not break her leg in the process. A small miracle. Thank God I was at work and only found out about this after it was all over, and everyone was safe.

Meow-Meow paid John back a little while later. Again, I avoided this adventure by being at work. John was sleeping upstairs in our room having worked the night before. Willie was not fully house-broken yet, so he was in a crate downstairs in a room that was under the new bathroom on the second floor.

Suddenly John was awakened by Meow-Meow on his chest frantically pawing and meowing. He pushed her away, but she wouldn't give up. She kept treading and butting him and was very vocal. By now John was awake and could hear water running. This was not right. He traced the noise and found a broken pipe in the new bathroom. The water was running so fast that it was now pouring into the floor below. The dog was getting wet and water was coming through a light fixture in the dining room. If the cat hadn't awakened John, there would have been more damage than what had already been done. Our little Meowser earned her keep that day.

But my favorite house renovation story involved the new shower stall. Again, I missed all the excitement by being at work (I'm no dummy!).

There were four bedrooms upstairs in John's wonderful dream house in Lehman. And one teeny tiny bathroom. This

38

bathroom contained a sink, a toilet and a bathtub but the room itself was so small that the door didn't open all the way. It bumped into the side of the tub. It was clear that someone along the way had just closed off the end of the hallway and turned it into a bathroom. So, John decided to make that bathroom a laundry room instead. This was ideal - a laundry room on the second floor. No more trudging laundry up and down stairs. Instead, he would make the smallest of the four bedrooms into our new bathroom. And because it was going to be so large there was room for a big Jacuzzi tub. Part of the renovation included a separate shower stall. We chose a one-piece molded model from one of the home renovation stores in town. The day of delivery arrived but they delivered the wrong color. John had a heated argument with the delivery people and after a loud telephone discussion with the store manager, it was decided a new shower stall would be delivered the next day.

Much to John's embarrassment, the newly delivered, correct color shower stall would not fit through any of the house doors. So, there it lay on the side lawn while John decided what to do. Ever the innovator, John got out that trusty ladder, the same one he had used to rescue Meow-Meow and placed it up alongside the house wall that was to be the bathroom. Then he got out his saws-all and made a hole in the wall big enough to slide the shower stall through. By using a system of rope pulleys, he managed to get the shower stall into the bathroom. Except now he had a huge hole in the wall over where the tub was going to go. But John had a plan. He had been carrying around two beautiful stained-glass windows for several years. They were originally from a demolished old building in Wilkes Barre and John had made them into a room divider when he lived in the Dallas house with his ex. Now they were just being stored in the attic until we decided what to do with them. They fit the hole in the wall perfectly. When that bathroom was finally finished, it was beautiful beyond my imagining. John built a large enclosure around the tub, big enough for plants and wine glasses. With the stained-glass windows shining down on us it was like bathing in heaven.

Chapter Four

CS

I learned early on that life with John was going to be an enjoyable ride no matter how I looked at it. John just loved life and saw the humor in just about everything. And he was a truly kind man. He loved me unconditionally and without fail and I never doubted that for a minute. Looking back, there are so many examples.

I had to have a hysterectomy in 2004 at the age of fifty-six. I had been having troubles for a while and was glad to have the surgery. I elected to have the procedure done laparoscopically which meant the doctor did it through a small incision in my abdomen. I didn't want to know how he could get everything out through that small hole. Best I slept through all that. But to do that kind of surgery, it's necessary to inflate the abdomen with gas. The idea is that most of the gas is expelled prior to the doctor sewing up the incision and whatever gas is left is supposed to be minimal and will get absorbed by the body over the next couple of days.

What they don't tell you is that you will have pain from that retained gas, it will be referred to your shoulder (meaning that is where you will feel it), and it will hurt like a son of a bitch! My pain started on the day after surgery, right after I was discharged, and as we were driving home from the hospital. Every so often I would wince in pain and lean forward. It felt as if a gladiator had run me through and it was hard not to yell out loud.

When we got home, I settled down on the sofa in the living room with a blanket and our animals, and John waited on me. He always made me feel so cared for. Between John's care and some ibuprofen, I remained comfortable with only an occasional bout of pain. The problem came that night. We had a waterbed back then and because of its construction I knew I would be in trouble if I slept in it. The bed had a frame that held the mattress. To get in or out (especially out), I would have to lean heavily on the frame to boost myself onto the floor. There was no way I could do that in the condition I was in. Any pressure on my arms caused the shoulder pain to come back with a vengeance.

So, I opted to sleep on the sofa that night. It was large and very comfortable. I assumed John would sleep in our bed even though that meant we would be separated. Imagine my surprise when I awoke during the night to find him asleep on the hard tile floor next to me in the living room. He was wrapped in a blanket, his head on a pillow he had taken from our bed.

He stirred and woke up when he heard me moving around.

"Are you all right? Do you need anything?" he asked.

"I'm good. But why are you sleeping on the floor? Why aren't you in bed?"

"I was afraid I wouldn't hear you if you needed me."

I think that is just about the most romantic thing John ever did. My heart melted. How lucky I was to be that loved by this wonderful man. But that was how John was. He always made me feel that I was the most important person in the world to him. I just knew I was.

He proved that another time when I became ill with bronchitis. It was December 7, 2000. My voice was getting more

I Will Never Leave You

and more hoarse as the morning hours went by. I had stayed home from work and was on the phone with one of my co-workers who had called to see how I was. I was in our bedroom on the phone with Kristin when John brought me in some soup. Then he went back into the kitchen. While I was talking to my friend my voice just went away and I was barely able to get out a whisper. I said good-bye to Kristin and took another sip of soup but by then even the soup felt scratchy in my throat. In fact, by this time my entire throat felt as if it was on fire. I knew something just wasn't right, so I got up and went to the kitchen to put the soup in the sink. At that time John was on the phone with a friend of his so I turned away. I did not want to interrupt him while trying to clear my throat. In that instant, I felt my throat "catch" and immediately seize up. Every time I tried to inhale, I felt as if my throat was slamming shut. I wasn't getting any air and I knew I was in trouble.

I turned to John and banged on the countertop to get his attention, all the while making a horrible loud wheezing noise. John looked at me, almost not comprehending what was happening. I pointed to the phone and banged on the countertop again. Only a couple of seconds had gone by, but it felt like an eternity. John sprang into action. He hung up and immediately dialed 911. Within minutes, we heard the ambulance arrive and the paramedics did their thing. By the time they arrived the spasms had subsided, and I could breathe although I still couldn't talk. They took me to the Emergency Room for treatment with John following in our car. The same episode happened again in the ER and John told me later that he was afraid they were going to have to intubate me. My oxygen levels dropped to a dangerous level but again with medication and breathing treatments the doctors got me well enough to discharge home.

However, John and I were both very shaken by what had happened. I was terrified to be alone. John called in sick from work for two days so he could be by my side. He knew I was traumatized (as was he). That just shows how John was. I didn't have to even ask. He just knew what I needed and there was never a doubt in my

43

Joy Collins

mind that I would be loved and cared for.

I have so many other loving memories too. None of them would probably matter to anyone but me but they all proved to me how our love and our life meant everything to John.

Here are some random examples:

I have always been an anxious person and could probably win an award for worrying. Over the years, John's even nature had a positive influence on me, but it was a struggle in our first years together. To help me remember that life was not an everyday battle John would take my pointer finger and draw a smiley face on it in ballpoint ink. ☺

Our Golden Retriever Jessie was going deaf in her later years and I taught her some sign language so we could continue to communicate. Nothing fancy. Some of it was real ASL sign language and some of it I even made up, but the hand signals meant something to Jessie and that's all that mattered. It got the job done. I taught the signs to John too and he became interested in learning others. We found the sign for "I love you" and it became our thing – we would sign "I love you" to each other whenever one of us left the house. John made sure to do it every time he left for work.

Early in our relationship, John bought a second-hand washing machine for me for my apartment so that I wouldn't have to go to the laundromat. The washer needed a little work, but John could fix anything. And of course, he came back with a story. He always did. He seemed to have a knack for meeting interesting people. Or maybe interesting people just opened up to him. Anyway, the man who sold John the washing machine had a pet raccoon who took a shining to John while he was inspecting the machine before the purchase. Apparently, the raccoon was a bit of a kleptomaniac too because the owner told John some stories about how the raccoon made off with some of his tools and hid them in odd places. As it was, when John brought the machine home and set it up, we found

44

a connection for a pneumatic tool hidden inside the washing drum.

John injured his hand at work in January 2008. He was working as a rehab nurse and was helping a man who had had a stroke transfer from his bed to a chair. The man was large and unsteady on his feet and a couple of steps into the transfer he started to go down. John grabbed the patient so that he wouldn't hit the floor and in that instant, he felt something snap in his left hand. Despite my best efforts, John refused to go to the doctor and have it checked. He wrapped it and took anti-inflammatory medication. But every so often he would hit his hand a certain way and would see stars. The pain was intense at times. Still, he insisted it would heal on its own. Finally, after two months he gave in and under the auspices of Workman's Compensation he went to an orthopedic surgeon. The verdict was a torn ligament and the only treatment was surgery. In the meantime, John had been working on the floor in my office. Initially we had put down wall to wall carpeting in the third bedroom that I was using as office space. Why we thought that was a good idea with so many pets in the house is beyond me and why he let me choose a cream-colored carpet is even more bizarre. Rather than replace the carpet with more carpet, even a darker colored one, we decided to go with wood laminate instead. This way it would be permanent and easier to keep clean. Now, with surgery looming and a long recovery period after that, John didn't want me to have to live with the bare concrete floor for several months. So, my dear husband with his injured painful hand laid the flooring in my office the week before surgery. I think of that sacrifice and all that love every time I look at the floor and I know his love is still here with me.

Then there is the Christmas cookie exchange story. One of the first jobs I had after we moved to the Phoenix area was at a call center. I was the equivalent of the Ask-a-Nurse for several insurance companies. We nurses sat at our little cubicles with headsets eight hours a day and doled out health advice to the people who called in. I wasn't sure I would like the job when I applied but I actually enjoyed it and as it turned out the job was serendipitous. It was Michelle my cubicle mate at this job who introduced me to the book *The Celestine Prophecy* which became part of the catalyst for our spiritual journey. But I'm getting ahead of myself.

Christmas of that year our little group of nurses decided to have a cookie exchange. Each of us committed to baking several dozen cookies, then packing them in small zip-lock plastic bags, six cookies to a bag, equivalent to the number of us that was in the exchange. The day of the exchange everyone would get one bag from each of us and then go home with a nice assortment of cookies. Ever the overachiever, I set about my task, baking cookies from scratch all afternoon and packing them up. Then, I put all the little baggies in a shopping bag in the hall closet next to my purse so I would be sure not to forget them. My job was thirty miles away in morning Phoenix traffic, a forty-five-minute commute on a good day.

That night, at three in the morning, I came down with a migraine headache. This was nothing new. I got them often. I tapped John on the shoulder and he sprang into action. He knew what to do. We had been through this many times. I kept my medication – Imitrex pills – in my purse so that I would never be without them. So, John got up and got my pill for me. I took it and went back to sleep. I woke up at six that morning and went into the living room, intent on letting our dog Willie out so he could relieve himself in the back yard while I brushed my teeth. Willie was a border collie/black Labrador mix. Very intelligent. And resourceful. And never met a cookie he didn't like. In his half-awake state, John had forgotten to close the hallway closet when he had gotten my headache pills hours earlier. Willie saw his chance and had taken it.

The living room was strewn with half-eaten bags of cookies. In some cases, nothing but the zipper part of the baggie was left. Willie had gone through several bags. He must have thought he was in doggie cookie heaven. I was in a panic. I made sure Willie was okay and then turned to the mess in the living room. Now what was I supposed to do? I woke John up and told him what had happened.

We didn't know if we should laugh or cry. If it wasn't for the fact that the cookie exchange was in hours, it was kind of funny.

"Don't worry," John said. "It was my fault for leaving the door open. I'll fix it. You just go to work and leave this to me."

After I left for work, my sweetheart went to the grocery store and bought several sticks of refrigerator cookie dough. He came home and baked several dozen cookies, bagged them as I had done the day before, drove them to my job, and hand delivered them to me in time for the cookie exchange. No, they weren't as fancy as the ones I had baked but I had cookies to give out and that's what mattered. And when I told my co-workers what had happened, they were envious that I had such a thoughtful husband and that made those cookies even more special. Win/win for me. And extra points for John.

But that was John. He was never afraid to go the extra mile for us and his passion for diving in and doing what was needed never ceased to amaze me. Like the time Buster, our big orange goofy Maine Coon cat, got stuck in our waterbed. John and I had gone away for the weekend and we had a pet sitter check on the kids. This was before she started staying over at night. Sara would just come in three or four times a day and walk the dogs, feed everyone, and have general play time. Buster was a big scaredy cat and would often hide. Sara saw a lump under the covers in our bed so she didn't think anything of it even though she didn't see Buster for a whole day.

We came home Sunday evening and I found everyone except Buster. I searched high and low getting more panicked by the minute. Then, I found the lump in the bed. And the lump hissed when I touched it. I knew it was Buster. What I couldn't understand was why there was a distinctive odor coming from the bed and why he wasn't coming out. I started to peel back the layers of covers – comforter, then blanket, then top sheet. Still no Buster. By now I was seeing wet sheets. I was down to the bottom sheet and still no cat. The odor of urine and feces was very strong now and the sheets were soaked. I yanked back the sheets and mattress cover exposing

47

the waterbed mattress and a wet and smelly cat. In his fear, Buster had burrowed under all the bedding and had then gotten himself wedged in, unable to figure how to get himself out. He had been in there for over twenty-four hours. I couldn't imagine the panic he must have felt. He had urinated and defecated in the platform that held the mattress and had also punctured the water mattress in several places in his terrified attempt to free himself. So, a lot of the water I was seeing was from the bed itself. And boy, did it stink.

I yelled to John to help me. I quickly grabbed a towel and wrapped the cat in it. Whether he wanted it or not, Buster was getting a bath right then and there. But what about the bed? Was it ruined?

John quickly got to work on the bed while I attended to Buster. The bed had to be drained so John set up a system of hoses and drained the bed into the back yard. Once the mattress was out of the frame, he scrubbed the inside of it with disinfectant and then ran an ozone air purifier in it.

There was no way we were going to be able to sleep in our bed for at least a few days so we bunked in the guest room and prayed that all of John's work would save our bed. Luckily, it worked. John patched the mattress holes a couple of days later and we filled the bed up again. No leaks! And no odors. Buster recovered from his ordeal and we got our bed back. From then on, Sara made sure all noses were accounted for every time she came to check on the kids.

Finally, I have two stories that are my favorite "John stories." I think they were John's favorites, too. For many years afterwards all we had to say to each other was "use the rope!" or the "electric blanket story" and we both knew what each other meant. And every time we both laughed.

I will start with the "Use the rope!" story.

The first few winters that John and I lived in Arizona we vacationed up north, usually in Flagstaff or Sedona. Most of the rooms we stayed in had fireplaces, many in the bedroom. And we had also experienced that same fireplace ambience in the many honeymoon places we frequented while we lived in Pennsylvania. We thought the whole idea was very romantic. So, John, ever the renovator, decided he could build us a fireplace in our bedroom in our house in Fountain Hills. The room was certainly large enough. He decided to build it in the corner of the room opposite our bed. Because it would be so close to the structure of the house, he decided to use a zero-clearance firebox. I don't know a whole lot about these things, but it was a safety issue apparently and the chimney that he built would have a double lining. Remember this – it's important to the story.

The fireplace turned out beautifully. We used it often. The winter nights in Arizona can still be quite chilly. At Christmastime, we decorated the wall over the fireplace with a beautiful wreath and we hung stockings for everyone on the mantle.

One spring morning, I heard a scraping noise in the fireplace corner of the room. The cats seemed quite interested as well. After listening for a while, we determined that a bird had somehow found its way into the chimney and was trying to get out. I assumed it would be okay.

But the next morning the noise was still there, and it was now apparent that something was wrong. Maybe the bird was stuck. I was upset and turned to John.

"We have to help him," I said.

John looked at me. He knew where this was headed. "We" meant him.

"What do you want me to do?"

"I don't know but we can't just let him stay there. I can't bear to listen to him scramble like that and die."

John sighed. He knew my passion for animals and he knew he was going to give in eventually because I was not going to let this go. So, still in his bathrobe, he got out his ladder and climbed up on the roof. A few minutes later he came back with the report. It wasn't good.

"I can see him but I can't get to him. He's down at the bottom of the chimney between the two flues. I don't know what to do."

"Maybe if we lower something to him, he can climb out."

John looked at me as if I had lost my mind.

"Lower what? A branch? What can get all the way down there to him?"

And then it hit me. "A rope. Lower a rope. He'll climb out on that."

John laughed at me and just shook his head.

"Okay, Joy, whatever you say."

So, to humor me, my dear sweet husband climbed back up on the roof and lowered a rope down in between the two flues of the chimney and placed the far end near the bird.

He came back in and told me "There's nothing else I can do. Either he'll come out or he won't but I'm going back to bed." He left to go put his ladder back in the garage.

I sat on the hearth and listened to the poor bird's frantic attempts to fly out. Every so often I could hear the rope slap against the metal wall of the chimney. In desperation I called out "use the rope!" all the while praying that the bird would somehow figure it out. Miraculously a few seconds later I heard the rope moving but no wing flapping. I couldn't believe it. Could it be? The rope kept moving and I ran outside onto the deck to get a better view of the top of the chimney. Within seconds, a sooty bird emerged. He sat on the chimney top, ruffled his feathers, chirped and flew away.

I ran back into the house and met John coming back in. "It worked! It worked! He got out," I yelled.

The look on John's face was priceless. "You're kidding me."

"No, you did it. He's gone."

And then I told John what I had done. "It sounds weird but I actually prayed and told him to use the rope."

"What?"

"I told the bird to use the rope."

John laughed. The mental image of me yelling up to the bird through the fireplace was too much. But he was grateful that what he had thought was my silly idea worked. A life had been saved and he got to go back to bed without his wife bugging him.

50

Later that day he went back up and placed a screen over the chimney opening so no other birds would meet a similar fate.

Whenever we heard birds on the roof after that John would look at me and say "Use the rope" and laugh.

But my most favorite John story involved our electric blanket. This happened when we were still living in Pennsylvania where the nights could truly be brutal. And even though we had a wonderful heating system in that remodeled farmhouse, it was still chilly when we crawled into bed at night until our bodies warmed the sheets. My parents gave us an electric blanket one Christmas and it soon became one of our favorite possessions. Especially for John. He loved that blanket. Sometimes, he would turn it on about fifteen minutes before we went to bed so that the sheets would be toasty warm when we crawled in under them.

It was also around this time that we decided to try for a baby. My biological clock was pounding in my ears. I had just turned forty and convinced John that a baby was just what we needed. So, we set about in earnest to see what would happen. After a few months with no baby I started researching ways to help us along. One of the things I learned was that heat was not conducive to healthy sperm. Uh-oh. What to do about John's nightly love affair with his electric sperm-killing blanket? I was afraid he was never going to agree to giving up the blanket.

As I was making the bed one morning, the blanket came unplugged from the individual temperature controls. Yet they remained lit. The only difference was the blanket would not be heated. I hatched a plan. I made the bed as usual and slipped the control end under the mattress as if it were still connected. Each of us could still play with our dials. I wondered if John would notice anything. The first night went off without a hitch. Not a word from John about a cold bed. Or the next night. Or the next. I couldn't believe it. He did not even turn the blanket on before sliding into bed. I couldn't believe my luck.

Finally, one night a full two weeks later, we were lying in

bed talking before lights out. John rolled over and reached for his blanket control. "I'm going to turn this blanket down. It's getting too warm."

I lost it. I started laughing. I laughed so hard I couldn't stop or speak. I was literally rolling around in bed and every time I tried to explain to John what had just happened, I would start laughing all over again. John looked at me as if I had lost my mind.

Finally, I caught my breath and could compose myself.

"What is wrong with you?" John asked.

"I'm sorry, Babe. But I have a confession to make. Your blanket isn't connected. That dial won't do anything."

"What?"

"Well, you know how heat isn't good for sperm?"

"Yeah."

"Well, I was afraid that the blanket would hurt our chances of conceiving, so I unplugged it. I thought for sure you'd figure it out, but you didn't. It's been like that for two weeks now. And then tonight when you tried to turn it down, I couldn't take it anymore. Are you mad?"

By this time, John was laughing too. "Mad? No, I'm not mad." He grabbed me. "You're crazy and I love you."

Chapter Five

CB

As I keep saying, life with John was nothing if not fun. With him I learned to enjoy everything for what it was.

Even working.

In late 1987, John and I embarked on a whole new chapter in our working life. We left our jobs as psychiatric nurses and joined the scores of nurses who were working only weekends and getting paid for full-time. It was too tempting a deal to pass up. The hitch was we had to work every weekend and we had to travel over two hours to get to these jobs, but we thought the upside was worth any downside. We made boatloads of money and we got to enjoy five days off in a row each week.

And thanks to our sense of humor we could get through some weird moments as well. This was also still during the time that we were trying to have a baby. Over the course of the next few years we worked at many different facilities that hired us strictly to work weekends. In addition to the great salary, we often enjoyed other perks such as being put up at the facility at no cost to us or being given meals at the hospital at their expense. Consequently, we slept in some strange places (hospital rooms, student dorm rooms) and ate lots of hospital cafeteria food. Yum!

But imagine trying to make love at the prescribed time in a single hospital bed with rails and controls? I guess it could have been kinky. I just thought it was awkward.

One assignment didn't provide sleeping quarters, so we arranged for the same room at a local motel every weekend at a reduced rate. At this hospital, we worked every Friday and Saturday from three in the afternoon until seven the following morning – sixteen-hour shifts. So, we only needed the room on Saturdays from about seven-thirty in the morning until about two that same afternoon. It was a strange little room behind a gas station. We had to cover the windows to block out the sunlight and it was often cold, so we slept under our coats until the heat kicked in.

And as I said these jobs were in cities far from home – Trenton, Stroudsburg, Hershey. Driving home on Sunday morning after a sixteen-hour shift was challenging. Most times, though, John managed fairly well. But there were some days he was just too sleepy, and I would take over. I remember one trip home where I just kind of zoned out and kept driving north, totally missing our exit. John woke up at one point and realized what I had done.

"Joy, where are we? You missed our exit."

Instead of agreeing, I became angry. "No, I didn't." I was sleepy and annoyed that John would even hint that I was wrong.

"Uh, Joy, you did. We're headed to Scranton (we lived south, outside of Wilkes Barre). We have to turn around." But instead of being upset, John was laughing at me. I was so determined that I was still headed the right way.

"I'm awake now. I can drive from here."

By this time, I knew he was right. "Sorry."

"It's okay." But John never let me forget what I had done. He thought my reaction was funny and never tired of retelling that story. Who knows where we would have wound up if he hadn't woken up just then.

54

Another time, we left work during a snowstorm. The snow had started during the night and roads were treacherous. We had been offered a hotel room to sleep in that day by the hospital with the incentive that they wanted us to work another shift that evening. I only wanted to get home. I was tired and I missed our bed and our animals. I convinced John to take us home. So, we headed out. By the time we got to the interstate the snow had stopped and driving wasn't so bad. The roads weren't plowed very well but we were making good time. We wondered why there wasn't anyone else on the interstate highway though. But we chalked it up to the time – it was early Sunday morning. Maybe people just weren't up yet. It was only when we got off at our exit that we found out the highway had been closed! Thank God, we didn't run into trouble. No one would have found us. That was before the days of cell phones.

John taught me life was to be lived and loved. In later years, we would often turn to each other and just suddenly say "I love our life". And we meant it.

We knew we were soul mates. Not in the trite way that people sometimes say, meaning they got along with their partner. We truly felt we had been destined for each other and that we had been together before.

There were some low points to be sure but no matter what life threw at us, we became stronger in our commitment to each other. I suffered some miscarriages. We lost some pets. John's relationship with his children was marred by some of the aftereffects that some divorces experience and eventually he became estranged from them.

Then we had some health challenges. Most notably, John had skin cancer twice and then prostate cancer. But again, we weathered the storms.

The biggest difficulty came when John's heart started to act up. First his heart rate was too fast, and we wound up in the Emergency Room a couple of times while they attempted to get him back in regular rhythm. Once they stopped his heart medically for a fraction of a second and it was so hard to watch John slip away and then come back a second later. Maybe it was a sign of things to come. But the medication worked, and we assumed we were out of the woods.

But that was not to be. The following year, John's heart rate went in the opposite direction. This time it was beating too slowly. I received a call from one of the nurses that John was working with telling me that he was in trouble. Yes, my Love was working and telling himself that all would be well despite his symptoms. In the meantime, his heart rate was creeping down into the 60's and he was starting to feel funny. I quickly drove to HealthSouth Rehab Hospital and picked him up and we drove to the Scottsdale Hospital Emergency Room again. This time they determined he needed a pacemaker. That seemed to do the trick. That was in March 2009. Unbeknownst to us we only had fourteen months left together.

Chapter Six
℘

In the early morning hours of May 24, 2010, John slipped away from this world and went on to his next adventure. Only this time it was without me.

No, that's wrong. It's still our adventure. John's favorite saying was "Things are happening the way they are supposed to." Sometimes he said it so much, he would laugh at me, knowing it would get under my skin.

But it was true and I knew it and he knew I knew it.

John and I considered ourselves spiritually ordinary in our early years together. I was raised Roman Catholic with all the guilt associated with that kind of thinking. John was raised Protestant but in no specific faith. We both believed in God and an Afterlife. Then I had a breast cancer scare and I went back to confession after a lapse of about twenty years. I started going back to Church on Sundays and John accompanied me.

Then my first husband died, and I started pushing for John

to get an annulment so we could be remarried in our Church. During the annulment process we found out that John had never been baptized so our Church wedding ceremony took on a life of its own. John was now going to convert to Catholicism and he was going to be baptized, confirmed and receive his First Holy Communion at the same time our marriage was going to be blessed.

All of which brought back a childhood story. When I was in the first and second grades at St. Francis of Assisi grammar school in Astoria Queens, the nuns collected quarters from us on various occasions. It was for the missions. One nun dubbed it money to save the "pagan babies". You know, those poor heathens who needed baptizing. What did I know? I was six.

Anyway, when we found out that John had never been baptized, I finally understood. "You're my pagan baby!" I told him. "You're the one I was donating money for."

See how the Universe works?

I wish I could say we had other revelations after that but we didn't. Life went along rather boringly, in the spiritual sense.

Until 1994 - that year we were talked into joining a multi-level marketing company by some dear friends of ours. It was a company that was headquartered in Japan and consequently run by Japanese principles. We didn't make much money selling the products but we were totally in love with the philosophy of the leaders. Although they didn't call it that, we were being introduced to ideas that we later understood to be the same ones that were made famous in the book and movie *The Secret*. We started reading Wayne Dyer and Deepak Chopra. We saw films by Gregg Braden. As I mentioned earlier, my friend at work introduced me to *The Celestine Prophecy*. After I read it, I gave it to John to read. He loved it. We both also read *Autobiography of a Yogi* by Paramahansa Yogananda. We learned to get in touch with our guardian angels. We even learned their names. Mine was Stephen and John's was Christopher. We talked about the afterlife and reincarnation. Over the course of sixteen years, we were gradually transformed.

John and I enjoyed our spiritual talks and sometimes we

experienced some truly odd occurrences. Two particularly strong incidences come to mind.

One Sunday I was attending the 5 P.M. Sunday Mass alone. John was home asleep. I don't remember why – perhaps he was not feeling well or maybe he was sleeping in preparation for working the night shift. It doesn't matter. However, at the end of the "Our Father" during Mass it is customary for the people in the congregation to turn to one another and offer each other a Sign of Peace. Usually it's a handshake and a simple "Peace be with you". John and I always hugged and told each other "I love you" before we turned to others. That Sunday I was missing John so I told my Guardian Angel to kiss John for me while he slept. By the time I returned home John was up and in our bathroom freshening up.

"Did you sleep okay?" I asked him.

John smiled, clearly enjoying himself. "Yes, I did until you came in and woke me up with a kiss. That was very nice."

I couldn't believe what I was hearing. "John, that wasn't me."

"What do you mean? Of course, it was. You kissed me. I felt it. It woke me up."

"I asked Stephen to give you a kiss for me because I was missing you at Church. This is the first time I have been in this room all afternoon. It wasn't me."

We were both amazed at what had happened.

The second incident was even more dramatic. This requires some background. I have believed for many years that at some point in my past (think previous lives) I have either been a race car driver or at the very least, I drove a stick shift. Mind you, I do not even know how to drive a stick shift in this life. Never learned and don't care to. All my cars have had automatic transmissions. Yet, there have been times when I have been cruising along, bopping to some good music, and suddenly I would find myself reaching for the clutch with my left foot and grabbing the gear shift with my right hand as if to shift the car. It has always been a smooth reaction, a natural body movement. In addition, I have often had a vague feeling of being in a car crash, possibly fiery and life-ending. In fact, once when I was in this mode, I heard ambulance sirens and started to pull over to let it go by only to realize that there was no ambulance in sight.

So, back to my story.

John was diagnosed with skin cancer in October 2007. This was his second occurrence and the lesion – located on his left shoulder – was rather large. We were both worried. John was scheduled for surgery to be performed in the doctor's office in Scottsdale. On October 23, 2007, at a little after Noon we headed out for the surgeon's office. We were in John's car and he was driving. We were barely out of our home town of Fountain Hills when his car's engine started to make some funny noises. Naturally we were worried that something was wrong. The plan was for me to drive us home after the surgery and if something bad happened with the car John would be unable to help. We decided to turn around and return home to get my car. Twenty minutes later we were back on the road. This time I was driving and John made a quick call to the doctor's office on his cell phone letting them know what had happened and that we were on our way. If all went well, we would still arrive on time.

A few minutes later, we approached the light at 56th Street and Shea Boulevard, a major cross street. There were three lanes of traffic going in both directions with an extra lane for turning. I was at the light in the middle lane heading west on Shea with one car – a white compact - ahead of me. The light turned green and I proceeded into the intersection. Suddenly, a school bus from the opposite direction and in the turning lane turned into our path. The driver was clearly turning against the light and I had no idea why he was. All I knew is that we were going to hit him head on.

I saw the bus hit the rear of the car in front of us and his bumper went flying.

I saw nothing but yellow in front of me and then my body just kicked in. From somewhere in my head I heard "You have done this before." My left foot shot out and hit the brake. My right hand grabbed the shift and I downshifted. I grabbed the steering wheel and gave it a hard right and then hit the gas. Then I quickly swerved left again. The car felt fluid in my hands as if it was gliding around the front of the bus.

All the while I kept hearing that voice in my head. "You're fine. You'll be OK. You've done this before."

And somehow…somehow…our car came to a stop in the middle of the intersection and the now stopped bus was behind us. The white car was at the far-right curb and the pissed off driver was standing next to it. But John and I were never hit. Not a scratch on the car or us.

John looked at me and his eyes were as big as saucers.

"What did you do?"

"I have no idea. I just went into my race car mode (John knew about my stick shift flashes) and drove."

We made it to the surgeon's office with time to spare.

When we got home, I started John's car. The noise was gone. The car ran fine and we never had a problem with it after that.

Things happen the way they are supposed to.

And sometimes we got carried away and read too much into things.

Like the time I was working as Head Nurse on a local psych unit and needed to be available to my staff on off hours. So, I carried a beeper (again this was before cell phones became routine). The idea was they would page me when they needed me and I would call the unit to see what I could do to help. This particular Saturday night I put the pager on vibrate and placed it on my dresser as John and I headed to bed. It was late and I didn't anticipate any calls. John and I spent some time chatting and then lights out. Before either of us dozed off we heard a slight hum in the room.

"John, you hear that?"

"Yeah."

"What do you think it is?"

"I don't know."

We had been talking a lot about spirits and communication

that week.

"Do you think it could be – I don't know – a spirit?"

"Maybe."

By this time, we were both wide awake and I turned on the bedside light.

"Maybe if we talk to it, it will go away."

So, we both got up and started talking out loud to this spirit who was somehow trying to communicate to us. I even went outside to see if I could see anything. I have no idea what I thought I would find. But when I came back in John was laughing and holding my pager.

"I found the spirit. He wants you to call work."

Sometimes a pager is just a pager.

Yet, the metaphysical was no stranger to me. I often felt that I was "different". My earliest recollection of being able to tap into something I didn't yet understand happened when I was about nine years old. I was living with my family in Astoria. My father worked as a sheet metal worker for Republic Aviation. For reasons my young mind didn't understand (and still don't today), Daddy was sent out to California with a group of his fellow workers to work on a plane in the Mohave Desert. He had been gone for several weeks and we missed him. It was the end of February and Daddy was due home the following week. My younger sister and I were playing in bed on a Saturday morning. Our mother wasn't up yet and I was amusing June by telling her stories.

The talk got around to Daddy being gone and my sister asked me when he was coming home. I thought a moment and in my mind's eye I saw another plane go down.

"Daddy's not coming home right now. Another plane went down and he has to stay and fix that one too."

My sister of course got upset but I stuck to my story.

Later that day a letter arrived from my father telling us that he was not coming home as he had hoped. Another plane had gone down and been damaged and he and his crew were going to stay and work on that one too. My sister looked at me but I didn't say a word. I was scared to death that what I had said that morning merely to amuse – and annoy – my sister was true.

I don't remember any other instances like that until after I graduated from nursing school. Then it was just little things, like knowing when someone was going to call or who was at the other end of the phone when it did ring, sensing when something was going to happen or not happen, and knowing in my heart if someone was telling me the truth. Soft little things like that, nothing major. But I trusted my gut a lot.

Then there was The Lady in Blue. This occurred when I was Head Nurse of a psych unit at a small free-standing psychiatric hospital in Wilkes Barre. It was the Children's Unit, to be specific. And the hospital was very old, housed in a building that had been used as a medical-surgical hospital in its heyday. We heard many ghost stories from our patients and believed very few of them. But some were consistent and told by patients over a long period, often by patients who had spent no time together so they could not have shared these stories.

A favorite was the lady in blue, as the children called her. They claimed a woman came to them at night and told them to behave and everything would be all right. They described her as wearing old fashioned clothing, most often a long blue dress. One day, everyone was at lunch and I was using the staff bathroom. It was a small unisex bathroom at the end of the hall facing the dorm rooms. As I emerged, I saw a woman walking ahead of me down the hallway. She didn't say anything and went into one of the patient rooms. I only got a quick glimpse of her but had the impression she was wearing a long blue dress. I thought nothing of it at the time except for the fact that no one was supposed to be on the locked unit except me. I called out to her but got no response. I followed her into the room I had seen her step into – and found myself alone! There was no one there.

I had seen the lady in blue. It shook me up and I was a believer after that.

63

Years passed and life was pretty ordinary. Until that fateful day when I was talking to Michelle my cubicle mate and she told me about some of the great metaphysical books she was reading and especially *The Celestine Prophecy* by James Redfield. John wasn't a big book reader but he devoured that one. It spoke to him for some reason. He was especially interested in the part about the Mayans and how they just seemed to disappear one day. John believed the book's theory that they just vibrated into another dimension.

The following year I took a job as Head Nurse on a Geriatric psych unit at one of the local hospitals in Mesa, Arizona. As luck would have it, I met a woman there who changed my life and helped me along on my spiritual journey. Sherri was very metaphysical and opened my mind to many possibilities. Through her I became more in touch with the angels in my life and shared that information with John. He in turn developed a relationship with his own angel.

A few years later, John and I were at dinner with our friend Shelley. It was the Christmas before John passed. Shelley was a strong believer in the same spiritual/metaphysical things that we were and we always enjoyed talking with her. During the conversation, John spontaneously told Shelley, "This is it for me. I'm done. After I go, I'm not coming back again."

Around the same time, I started having strange "feelings". I didn't want to call them premonitions because they were too scary to give them that much importance. But I remember looking at John's foot one evening. We were watching television in bed and John had stuck his right foot outside the covers. I just stared at it. For some reason, it caught my eye.

Then another night, I was snuggling next to him while we watched TV (we did that a lot) and tried to make a connection to him with my mind. I never told John about that. Even I thought I was being weird but I remember it felt important to me to try.

John often teased me about the way I slept. I had a funny way of holding my hands that he found endearing. When these "feelings" started to pop up I noticed I was often holding my right hand across my chest as if I had had a stroke. It happened often enough that I was acutely aware of it and would move my hand away because it made me uncomfortable. It was around this same time that I started having thoughts about what I would do if John were to die. I dismissed them as the kind of odd thoughts that married couples might have. It certainly wasn't something that was going to happen to us.

Until the day I walked into our bedroom and saw John asleep. He was halfway turned on his side with his head leaning toward his right, his mouth drooping a little. My heart stopped. He actually looked as if he had passed. I could see him breathing so I knew he was all right but the look on his face unnerved me and I nudged him so that he would move.

Then our friend Shelley, whom I mentioned before, sent me an email on May 12, 2010, containing a very descriptive document called "Through the Light - The Near-Death Experience of Mellen-Thomas Benedict". It went into detail about the experiences this particular gentleman had had while apparently deceased before he came back to life. After I read it, I shared it with John and he loved it. It had a profound effect on him. He couldn't stop talking about it. The timing was eerie. Twelve days later, John was gone. In fact, the night before, just hours before John transitioned, we were riding the Long Island Railroad with my cousin Claudia heading back into the city – John and I to our hotel and Claudia to her apartment. Somehow, we got onto the topic of death and John told Claudia about the article Shelley had sent us. It had made that much of an impression on him.

All these thoughts came flooding back to me after John passed. When I found John, the first thing I saw was his foot as I approached the bathroom door. It was that foot that told me something was terribly horribly wrong because it was too close to the door and it was mottled and discolored. And when I pushed the door open and saw John, his face was the mirror image of how he had been in bed the day I nudged him awake because he looked dead and his arm was held in the same way I had held my arm when I creeped myself out. My soul had been trying to prepare me for what was soon to happen.

Those last days were prophetic in other ways as well. John finally finished a major house renovation that he had been idling with for a couple of years. We were updating both bathrooms – retiling, new floors, new paint – and John had been doing a little at a time whenever he could. But in April he put a big push on and finished them both completely. We also redid our pool and John even went in it once. He loved our pool.

Then that Sunday, our last day together, we were visiting family out on Long Island. Somehow the after-dinner conversation turned to everyone's cholesterol level. I had just gotten mine back and as usual it was high. I don't tolerate statin medications very well so my plan was to look into alternative treatment. John was concerned though.

"Make sure you take care of this, Joy. I don't want to be here without you."

Of all the things to say, why did he say that? And why did he say that just hours before he passed?

Then, that night, as we snuggled together in the bed in our hotel room, we talked about how good it would be to get on the plane and head home to Arizona.

"I'm looking forward to going home," John said.

Little did we know…

Chapter Seven
CB

And that was my life with John – happy, funny, loving, complete, spiritually uplifting, my entire world.

And now it seemed to be over and I was in a dead silent hotel room.

John was gone.

The Front Desk clerk had left to go back to the lobby and wait for the paramedics.

I went back into the bathroom and hugged and kissed John. I couldn't stop crying. Yet, in all my misery I knew he was still with me, hovering. I sat in the armchair and talked to him and told him exactly how I felt about what had happened.

"I know we agreed to this, John. I know this was the plan but I have changed my mind. I want a do-over. Please come back. Please. I can't do this. I can't."

But nothing changed. John was still gone.

I remember only bits and pieces of the next twenty-four

hours. Once the poor Front Desk attendant left me to go meet the paramedics, I called my cousin Claudia who lived in the city. Remember we had been visiting my relatives in New York that weekend and had been scheduled to leave on our flight back to Phoenix just hours later. I don't remember what I told Claudia. Later, she told me she wasn't sure herself if she had heard correctly and in the cab on the way to meeting me at the hotel she checked her cell phone on the off chance that she had been dreaming. But there it was – irrefutable proof that I had called her with the horrible news.

While I waited for Claudia to arrive I called a friend back in Fountain Hills. It was three hours earlier in Arizona and Louise and her husband Jim hadn't gone to bed yet. At first Louise wasn't even sure who she was talking to. She later told me that all she heard was screaming and crying and my voice was unrecognizable.

I remember the crying. I remember hearing the sirens in the distance knowing they were coming for John and knowing there was nothing they could do. Eventually I could tell her what had happened. I remember telling her I wanted to die, throwing myself on the bed. I don't remember much more.

But I remember the sirens.

I will always remember the sirens. But unlike the phantom sirens when I was driving my imagined car with the stick shift, these were real.

The next few hours were a flurry of activity. Claudia arrived. The desk clerk came back with the paramedics who took one look at John and told me there was nothing they could do. Because of New York laws regarding unwitnessed deaths, the coroner had to be called to give his permission to remove the body. The desk clerk was kind enough to move me to another room to wait until the coroner arrived. While we waited, Claudia and I made more phone calls – another one to Louise and one to the mortuary in Arizona who assured us he would handle all the details so that he could bring John back home. We might have made other calls. I honestly don't remember.

Then the coroner came to my room to speak to me. He was

very kind and verified that there was no evidence of foul play and asked me if I wanted an autopsy. I couldn't bear the idea of cutting John open. Maybe in retrospect it would have been good to know why this had happened but it wasn't going to bring him back. I said no.

"Then just sign this release and we will have him removed to the Medical Examiner's Office. They will coordinate with a funeral home here to prepare him for transporting back to Arizona."

I signed the forms. "Can I see him before you take him away?"

"Of course, come with me."

Claudia and I went back to the room that just hours before had been so happy, so normal.

John was already on the floor inside a body bag, ready to be taken away. He was in full rigor and didn't even look like himself. I got on the floor and touched him, told him I loved him while the two attendants stood by and waited.

"Please take good care of him," I said.

They nodded and I left and waited outside the room with Claudia. The coroner came out and handed me John's medical alert bracelet that he wore because of his pacemaker.

In a few minutes, they wheeled the gurney with John's body, now zipped inside the big black bag, into the hallway and then into the waiting elevator. The reality of what I was watching became too much for me and I ran. I had no idea where I was going. I just ran. Eventually I came to the end of the hallway and had to turn around and came back. Claudia was still there, waiting for me along with the desk clerk. She hugged me.

Then we began the grim task of packing up the room. When we had finished, we checked out and headed back to Claudia's apartment and more phone calls. The sun was just coming up as we got into the cab. My new life without John by my side had begun.

Chapter Eight

CB

The next few hours somehow crawled by. There were things to take care of and somehow I managed. I think John was helping me from the Other Side because I can't believe that in the state I was in that I could get things done as well as I did. I do remember talking to John and telling him that I knew we were doing this together.

From the beginning, I knew in my heart that this was going to be our journey together, not just mine. The love we shared was strong and special and if any couple in the world could do this beyond the grave, so to speak, we were the ones who were going to do it. It wasn't just a feeling. It was a knowing deep in my soul.

One of the first people I had to call was John's Mom. Frances Collins was living in Denison, Texas where she and her husband had retired many years before. How was I going to tell her? How do you tell a mother that her son has died? We had just visited her the month before and John and I were both concerned with how frail she was becoming. She had had a small stroke the October before and was a little unsteady on her feet but was doing all right otherwise. Her mind still seemed sharp. But Mom had endured a lot in her life and had lost all her remaining family except for John in the last few years. Her younger son had died of a heart attack at the age of fifty-three in 2001. Her sister for whom she had been caregiver had passed away in a nursing home in 2004. Her husband, John's father, had died in 2008. John had been calling her every evening to check on her. It was their ritual that I know she looked forward to. They had spoken just the evening before. Now I had to tell her those calls were forever silenced.

I was afraid to just blurt the news to her over the phone especially if she was alone. I was afraid what the shock might do to her. Then somehow I remembered there was a family cousin Ron who lived in the same town (Thank you for helping, John). He also sold insurance so Claudia and I powered up her computer and did a search for his company. We found it quickly and copied the number. With the time difference, I knew we would have to wait a little while before we could call.

In the meantime, there were other arrangements to be made. I had a driving need to get back to our home, to our animals, to our bed so we changed my plane reservation to a flight for that afternoon. As the sun made its way over the country and rose in different time zones, I called various people to let them know what had happened. The mortuary in Fountain Hills told me John would be transported that day from the Medical Examiner to a funeral home in New York. They would prepare him for his flight back to Arizona, most likely within the next two days. I looked at John's suitcase sitting in Claudia's foyer. How could it be possible that it was going back to Arizona without him?

I don't think words can adequately describe how I felt that morning. I was going through the motions and getting things done but a part of my brain was in a fog and couldn't – wouldn't – believe that this was happening. How could I be calling people and telling them John had died? How could this be? We had been talking just hours before. We had plans. We were so happy. There had been no warning. None.

I couldn't eat. I couldn't rest. I had had no sleep since the time I had awoken and found John. I felt like I wanted to jump out of my own skin. I was crying almost non-stop and felt like I wanted to throw up. My heart was broken.

And then it was time to call John's Mom. I dialed Ron's office number and spoke to his assistant. I told her who I was. She didn't know me but knew the family and was very nice.

"Something terrible has happened," I said in between sobs. "I have to tell Frances but I don't want her to be alone when I do."

"What happened? What can we do to help?"

"Frances' son John died suddenly last night and I have to tell her but I am afraid what the news will do to her. Can you get in touch with Ron and see if he can be with her when I tell her?"

"Oh, my dear. I am so sorry. Of course, we'll help. Ron's not in the office yet but I'll call him at home and tell him. Give me your number and I'll call you back. Are you all right? Where are you?"

I couldn't believe how kind this stranger was being. I am sure part of it was because she was a friend of Frances but I also sensed part of it was just Southern hospitality and a female kinship at hearing such devastating news. That sense of caring was something I experienced over and over again in the next few days.

Ron called me back a few minutes later and I told him the story that I was now starting to repeat more times than I cared to. He promised to get in touch with Frances and be there for her when I told her. When they called me back about forty-five minutes later, he had apparently already told Mom that John had passed. I was a little surprised but it saved me from being the first to tell her the news. We cried together. I told her how sorry I was. Even in her sadness, Mom tried to comfort me, telling me she would be there for me.

It reminded me of the conversation we had had just weeks before when we were visiting her in Texas. It was our first night there and Frances had prepared a wonderful supper for us. She inquired about my parents. I looked at John. Things were not going well with my parents and I wasn't sure how much to say.

73

Actually, that was a gross understatement. My relationship with my parents – my mother especially – has been rocky my entire adult life. One time I remember being so upset with her I listed her as deceased on a hospital form.

Anyway, this latest dust-up had occurred earlier that month. John and I had talked about trips we wanted to take that year. We had been visiting his Mom every few months since his Dad had died but we hadn't seen my family in a few years. I had parents in Florida and an aunt and uncle whom I loved dearly who lived in New York. So, we decided we would visit my parents in May and then my aunt and uncle in the fall. And hopefully squeeze in a vacation for just the two of us in between. We already had the April visit to John's Mom planned.

I dialed my mother's phone number to let her know we wanted to visit. Imagine my surprise when I heard a whiny tone and then a recording: "We're sorry. The number you have dialed has been disconnected. If you have reached this number in error, please hang up and dial again."

Okay. I dialed again. Same whiny noise. Same recording.

I called my aunt.

"Aunt Mary, have you spoken to my Mom lately?"

"Not for a couple of weeks. Why?"

"Well I just called down there and their phone is disconnected. I'm wondering what's going on. Maybe they didn't pay their bill? I'm trying not to worry but this is awfully strange."

"Let me try. I'll call you back."

A few minutes later Aunt Mary called me back. "I got the same thing. Now I'm worried. I hope everything is all right. What could have happened?"

Over the next hour or so we contacted my brother who found out that my parents had sold their home and since they didn't have a new place to move into yet had moved in with my sister. Of course, no one bothered to tell me or my Aunt. And since I wasn't speaking with my sister (another story), I wasn't going to call my mother there.

But at least everyone was all right. And it was because of that episode that John and I decided to visit my aunt and uncle in New York in May instead of in the fall and that visit is when John passed.

"Things are happening the way they are supposed to."

But I'm getting ahead of myself.

Back to dinner with John's Mom and her question about my parents. In answer John said, "They moved and didn't bother to tell us. So, Joy hasn't spoken with them in a while."

Frances looked at me, disbelief obvious on her face. She knew my relationship with my mother was not perfect, but I guess even she didn't realize how bad it was.

I smiled weakly. "I guess I don't have a mother anymore."

Frances reached across the table and softly put her hand on my arm. "I'll be your mother," she said. I had no idea at that moment how prophetic those words would be. But they still touched me deeply.

And now, I had to explain to this woman who opened her heart to me that her son, her only living child, my husband, had died. I felt as if I had failed her.

Frances was tearful but she took the news better than I thought she would. I was grateful that she wasn't alone. She asked about my plans and I told her I was going back home that night and I would call her when I got home if it wasn't too late. Otherwise, I would call her in the morning.

After I hung up, I made a promise to John. "I know how much you love your Mom and how important it was to you to make sure she was all right. I promise as long as she and I are alive, I will care for her as you would have. I will make sure nothing bad ever happens to her. I promise you, Baby."

As I mentioned before, John had had a pacemaker inserted the year before due to a dangerously low heart rate. John's cardiologist was also a friend – more to John than to me – but I felt I should call and let Dr. Simonie know what had happened. Dr. Simonie was upset that I had decided not to have an autopsy. He wanted to know why John had died since we both suspected that it had something to do with his heart. According to John's medical records, he was in great health. This should not have happened. And yet, it did.

But Dr. Simonie had another plan.

"After they bring John back to Arizona, I will have the pacemaker rep go down to the funeral home and query the pacemaker. We can run a strip off the memory and see if that tells us anything." I was grateful for that information. Maybe we would learn something after all.

And soon, it was miraculously time to head out to the airport. Mercifully, Claudia went with me. I needed help maneuvering all the luggage, but I also needed the moral support. My flight was scheduled for 4:30 in the afternoon leaving out of Newark. With the time change, I would arrive in Arizona around 6:30 that night. I just wanted to blink my eyes and be home. I had no idea how I was going to get through an almost five-hour flight on my own.

It seemed so weird to be going home without John, to be lugging his suitcase around without him.

When we arrived at the ticket counter to check my bags, we got bad news. There was mechanical trouble with my plane and it was delayed an unknown period of time.

"You don't understand. She has to get home now," Claudia said. She explained the situation to the clerk. I'm sure the look on my face told her all she needed to know. To her credit, the clerk was more than understanding.

"I can get you on a flight on another airline, leaving at around the same time as your previously scheduled flight. You'll arrive almost at the same time as you would have on our flight."

"Great. Let's do that."

"Okay, I can check your bags here but the gate is in another terminal." She pointed to our right. "You'll have to go down those stairs and catch the tram."

I thanked the clerk. After checking my bags and getting my new boarding pass issued, Claudia and I ran for the stairs. And that was when John reached out to me for the first time since he had passed. As we were running down the stairs, overhead on the airport loudspeaker came the song "Lyin' Eyes" by the Eagles. I couldn't believe it.

Years ago, when I was divorcing my first husband, he dedicated that song to me. I'm not sure why. Bill did not take my decision to leave him very well. He felt that I was giving him a raw deal and was very afraid I was going to try to bilk him out of money. The opposite was true. My attorney had told me that I was the only doctor's wife he knew who got next to nothing in her divorce. I didn't care. I just wanted out. But that didn't stop Bill from being angry and so he tried to hurt me by telling me that "Lyin' Eyes" was my song since it was about a scheming wife who cheated.

I had told John about it when it happened and he helped me laugh about it. Over the years it became our private joke. Every time the song came on the radio, John never failed to poke me lovingly in the arm and say "There's your song, Joy." And he would smile and that would make me smile.

And now John was doing it again. He was poking me. He wanted me to smile. I couldn't believe it. Was it true? It had to be. I grabbed Claudia's arm.

"That's John," I said through tears. "He's here. He wants us to be happy." I felt anything but happy but it was comforting to know he was with me. Claudia squeezed my hand and we made our way to the tram.

We made it to the gate with plenty of time to spare. At one point, Claudia got up and left me to speak with the attendants at the check-in counter. I found out later she told them what had happened and asked them to pass on the word to the airline attendants to keep an eye on me during the flight. I don't know if they did or not. No one approached me during the flight, even though I sat there with tears streaming down my face a large part of the time. Not even my seat mate seemed to notice. I was quickly learning that sadness, especially when linked to a death, is something that people have a hard time dealing with and prefer to just ignore it, perhaps hoping it

Joy Collins

will just disappear.

     While Claudia and I sat at the gate, waiting for the boarding call for my flight, we tried to make the time pass by talking about the things that needed to be done when I got home.

     Suddenly, I realized I didn't have John's wedding ring and I had no idea where it was. He had been wearing it when he passed away. He always wore it; he never took it off. On those rare occasions when he did (usually involving surgery) I kept it for safekeeping and then I was the one who placed it back on his finger, kissing the ring before I did so. It was a ritual we did for each other. As I mentioned earlier, before the mortuary attendants took John from the hotel room earlier that morning, the coroner had given me John's Medic Alert bracelet. But no one had given me his ring and I had completely forgotten about it. Now I was in a panic, not knowing what had happened to it. I couldn't even think where to start.

     Claudia took over and started making phone calls. By now it was almost five o'clock and we knew offices would start to close soon. After a couple of calls, she had some leads and promised to follow up for me. From what we could piece together, John had his ring when he arrived at the Medical Examiner's office but not when he arrived at the funeral home. Hopefully it was someplace safe in between those two places.

     And then it was time to board.

Chapter Nine

CB

The flight home was uneventful and as soon as we landed, I was up and out of my seat. I wanted to be home, away from all this. To be in our house, with our furbabies (what I called our pets). I wanted to be alone to scream and cry.

But there were things to be done. And even as I made my way out of the plane, I started making the call that I would have to make over and over and over again, notifying everyone who needed to know to tell them John was no longer here.

Louise and Jim met me at the gate. The looks on their faces said it all. They were in as much disbelief as I was. This was a nightmare that would not end. Despite some initial confusion, we made our way back to the car that John had parked in one of the long-term lots just four days before. How life had changed since then!

Louise and I drove John's car home, with Jim following us

Joy Collins

in his car back to my house. Louise had called ahead and spoken to Amy, our pet sitter. Amy was also a family friend who in fact had known John before she even started taking care of our babies. Louise had told Amy what had happened and asked her to meet us at the house. The look on Amy's face when I walked into the house told me she had been crying. She hugged me and said that she had explained what had happened to the girls, meaning Toby and Jessie, our dogs. I sat on the floor and immediately the two dogs were all over me. I also noted that they didn't even look for John. Could it be that they understood what had happened? I hugged them close and my tears fell on their fur. I needed them so much. I knew I had made the right choice to come home so soon.

But I needed some space alone. I hadn't been alone since I had found John that morning. It seemed like eons ago now. I took the girls outside to go potty while Louise and Jim and Amy talked. I knew they were trying to decide what to do about me. On the way home, Louise had tried to get me to agree to let someone stay with me that night but I refused. I wanted to be alone. I needed time to think, to let this sink in, to just breathe.

So, for now it was just me and Toby and Jessie out under the stars.

I looked up. Was John there? Could he see me? Could he hear me? I felt so alone. I wanted to feel John, to know he was with me. But all I felt was emptiness.

One thing I had noticed as soon as I walked into the kitchen when I first came home was that the overhead kitchen light – made up of four fluorescent bulbs – was flickering. It had never done that before. Was that a sign? Or was I just looking for anything to make myself feel better? I had no idea.

But now as I walked back into the house, I looked at Jim leaning against the kitchen counter and the whole room seemed cloudy. I blinked my eyes, not believing what I was seeing. The mist was still there. And then as suddenly as it had appeared, it was gone. I chalked it up to being exhausted.

After a few more minutes of talking, I convinced everyone I

80

would be fine and they left.

I was now finally alone.

And I suddenly wasn't sure I wanted to be. I needed someone to talk to but who at this late hour?

Years before I had joined a second wives online support group. The large group had disbanded but a few of us kept in touch. We had formed a Yahoo email group. I got online and sent an email to the group:

"Is anyone up? Something really bad has happened and I need someone to talk to."

Within minutes, Karen emailed me back:

"I'm here. What can I do?"

I sent her my phone number. I just couldn't type what had happened.

I don't remember anything of that conversation. All I know is that Karen called me and we talked and cried together. She then emailed the rest of the group and told them what had happened. Those women kept me sane over the next few days. Up until that point I had only met one of them in person but in our mutual need we had all become friends. One by one over the course of that week, they called me and we cried together over the phone.

Having hung up the phone after talking with Karen, I knew it was time to try to get some sleep. The next few days were going to be very hard. I crawled into bed, unsure if sleep would ever come again.

And I dreamt of John. Weeks later, I learned that what happened that night was not a dream but a visit. John came back to me and we were able to say our good-bye. But that night I just thought it was a very vivid dream and I was thankful even for that.

Waking up alone in our bed was the worst feeling in the world. As soon as I opened my eyes and my head cleared, the reality of the last thirty-six hours hit me all over again. I reached over to John's side of the bed and just cried. How was I going to do this? This was not how we had planned our life to go. Was it possible that only two days earlier we had been having dinner with my family, laughing, taking pictures? Now just getting out of bed and breathing seemed like an insurmountable task. Luckily, the dogs needed to go out and be fed and if nothing else, I needed to get up and take care of them.

I took them outside in the back yard and mentally went over what I needed to do that day – calls, funeral parlor, flowers....

I called the paper and asked about the procedure to get his obituary in for the next day.

Next was the trip to the funeral parlor to plan for the viewing. Then to the florist to pick out flowers. I wanted something simple. I knew John wouldn't want a big fuss but there had to be something from me and I also picked out a small basket of flowers from our "kids" – the dogs and cats. They were our children and they loved him.

On Wednesday, I met with the organist at the Church and he helped me formulate the music for the Requiem Mass. John and I had always attended the Franciscan Renewal Center in Paradise Valley, affectionately called "the Casa" by those who loved it. It was run by Franciscan friars. The atmosphere at that church was always one of acceptance and love and they welcomed everyone. I knew it was the right place to have John's funeral. And I was right. Brian allowed me to choose music that meant something to John and me. I asked him if we could have our wedding song, Anne Murray's "You Needed Me". It was our song.

Brian knew the song. But he didn't feel comfortable singing it. "That is Anne Murray's signature song. I doubt I can do it justice. How about if I get a recording of it instead and play that? We can have it playing as people are gathering for the service."

I also wanted "To Where You Are", a song made popular by Josh Groban that summed up how I was feeling. To this day, every time I hear it, I get overwhelmed with emotion. Brian agreed and we rounded out the service with some more typical spiritual music that I thought John would like.

I wrote a short eulogy but I knew I would never be able to get through it if I read it myself so one of the women at the church read it for me.

And so, the week went and before I knew it, Friday afternoon arrived and the viewing and the funeral were over.

And John's body was at the crematorium and I was home alone.

Forever.

Now what?

PART TWO

DO

Learning how to continue our relationship

Chapter Ten

I had an insatiable urge to know what John was going through.

Where was he?

What was he doing?

Was he okay?

Was it true that he was still with me, communicating, loving me?

Could I contact him?

How could I find out the answers to these questions?

So, I turned to what I knew best – research. Years before John had teased me about the fact that I would try to learn everything I could about something before I experienced it. When we went to Disney World for the first time, I bought books on the park and had outlined the best rides and had even made routes from one to the other to minimize walking time and wait time and maximize our experience. I did that with everything. It was just the way I was.

But John found this endearing for some reason. In fact, he told me one day, "Joy, when you get to Heaven you are going to find two doors. One is going to say "Heaven" and the other one is going to say "Lecture on Heaven" and you're going to attend the lecture first." In fact, from then on, whenever I went into research about something, John would laugh and say "Lecture on Heaven" and we both knew what he meant.

So, this time, I *did* look for a lecture on Heaven.

I started by reading books on grief. Any books I could find. Somewhere there had to be the answer to what I was seeking.

But I didn't find it.

Instead, I found platitudes that didn't ring true. Books that told me when to give John's clothes away, when to take off my wedding ring, how exercise would make me feel better, how changing the décor of the house would make everything all right again. One stupid woman wrote about how wearing a new baseball cap changed her from grieving to hope.

Really?

A baseball cap was all it took to make you okay with losing the love of your life?

I remember literally throwing one book across the room because it annoyed me so.

I don't claim to have the market cornered on experiencing grief, but I do believe that losing a true soul mate is harder to endure than losing "just" your mate because not every marriage is between soul mates. I have known partners who sniped at each other every day, who ridiculed their spouses behind their back, who were out dating and partying mere months after losing their husband or wife. And I am not condemning those people. I am just stating that those were not marriages between soul mates.

And that's okay.

And, to be clear, my experience is mine and mine alone. I am the first to admit that. But I also think that there are certain qualities associated with being married to your true soul mate – or twin flame as some refer to it – and when that union is severed by death, the grieving process is far more difficult.

How do I define a soul mate? To me, a soul mate is someone you have been with not only in this life but in other lives as well in addition to being bonded between lives. When you meet your soul mate it's as if the search you didn't even know you were on is finally over. Everything just seems to fall into place. Your soul says "There you are!" And even through trials and hard times, nothing can separate you. In fact, the hard times just make you stronger.

Everything about the relationship is heightened. Even lovemaking is stronger, more intense. You feel as though you are finally home and safe. The connection is spiritual as well as physical. You are always in each other's thoughts and the welfare of the other is always uppermost. Even when you are apart, there is a feeling of "home" that you carry within you that makes you feel safe and cared for, knowing that the other is aware of you and cares deeply for you, and knows you like no one else on the planet does.

Two hearts, two bodies, two souls intimately and forever bonded.

When that special union is broken apart by death the sorrow is almost insurmountable; the level of devastation too hard to describe. It has been documented that our hearts as well as our brains send out electrical charges that extend far beyond our physical bodies. It is my belief that these electrical connections that our bodies make intertwine with the electrical connections of our soul mates, forming a unique bond. Our bodies physically feel the disconnection death makes. Our very auras are changed. No wonder we are so bereft.

I started journaling soon after John passed and I also started a blog that same summer. Here is some of what I wrote to describe my feelings of grief:

I've lost more than my husband, my mate. I've lost my best friend, the person I could count on for everything no matter what. The person I trusted my life and soul with. The person I knew would always do right by me, who loved me unconditionally, and cared deeply about me above all else, even above himself. You don't just forget that. You don't "move on". There is no getting over that.

The enormity of John's gone-ness is only just beginning to sink in and as it does, the grief deepens. It soaks into me, becomes a part of me. It doesn't define me. I am still me. But now I am me, grieving. I will always be me grieving. When I laugh, I will wish John could share it with me. When I cry, I will wish he were there to hold me. When I enjoy something, I will wish John could enjoy it with me. I will never be able to do anything with him physically in this world again and the magnitude of that shatters me.

How long does grief last?
That's a trick question.
Grief never ends.
It evolves and transforms you, but it is never over.
Maybe if you are grieving a spouse and you remarry, maybe that is the ultimate transformation of grief. Although I am sure even then you don't stop grieving the spouse you lost.
Maybe it becomes more compartmentalized.
But I don't know. I can't speak from experience regarding that because I have not remarried.
And I don't ever intend to.
John and I are soul mates, twin flames, one half of an awesome whole. Any married relationship I could have at this point in my life would be a poor aftermath. It could not ever live up to what John and I had and still have, although it's now changed.
Marriage to John was my home, my refuge, my strength, my comfort, my love. It is only now that John is no longer physically here that I am just beginning to realize how overwhelmingly much we meant to each other and how much we permeated each other's lives.
We were Johnandjoy, never apart - not spiritually, not emotionally, and hardly ever physically. We worked together, we played together, we loved together. We were constantly in each

other's thoughts - and sometimes even knew each other's thoughts.

We knew our life was good and we appreciated it.

We knew what we had was special.

But as with everything else that is there before you every day, you just assume it will always be there.

Losing John to death leaves me absolutely bereft.

The sadness and loneliness is overwhelming at times, even after two years.

And this sadness of grief is not something that really goes away. Yes, it changes. I don't cry every day. I hardly ever scream any more or pound the furniture in the frustration of grief.

But I ache in my heart.

Constantly.

Every day.

I yearn for what was.

I see couples going about their day and I feel cheated.

Nothing brings true lasting joy any more.

Every day I am reminded that John's not here.

John's not here.

John's.

Not.

Here.

How long does grief last?

Forever.

I found just getting through a day to be extremely difficult. If it weren't for the fact that I had to feed our fur-children I probably wouldn't have even gotten out of bed. I dragged myself through the days as if walking through deep mud. I would start something – like making the bed – and then get distracted or overwhelmed and forget what I was doing. Hours later, I would walk back into a room and find something that I had abandoned – a cupboard open, a glass on a counter, the bed half-made.

Mercifully, somehow the day would end but I had no idea where it went. I lost my appetite and dropped fifteen pounds in just a few weeks. I couldn't sleep, often waking up every night at the exact time that I had found John gone. I had horrible flashbacks of finding him that caused me to scream out in agony and started long crying jags.

One consolation was recovering John's wedding ring. All that week after John passed, my cousin Claudia had been working to track down John's ring. He had it on when they took him from the hotel room. I thought perhaps rigor prevented them from being able to remove it. In any event, it was recorded as being on him at the Medical Examiner's office but he was not wearing it when he showed up at the funeral home in New York prior to being prepared for his flight back to Arizona.

After several phone calls, it was determined that some "property" was logged in at the ME's office but it was unknown what it was. I just knew it had to be his wedding ring. More phone calls and now they wanted paperwork signed and notarized so that Claudia could retrieve whatever it was.

Another couple of days went by. More emails. Fed-exing of paperwork. And then came the blessed confirmation. Claudia not only emailed me that she had John's ring but she texted me a picture of it. I cried when I saw it. Having the ring that he wore for almost twenty-nine years meant everything to me.

Claudia promised to guard it with her life and rather than chance it to the postal system she promised to hand carry it with her when she would come to see me in a few weeks.

That summer was the worst of my life. Luckily, I had friends that helped. Between my two cousins and some friends, they all took turns coming out and spending weekends with me. I wish I could say I remember what we said or did but I don't. It's all a blur and will probably remain so.

And maybe, it's just as well. Who wants to remember the darkest days of their life?

Miraculously though, I managed to get things done.

The most important thing I felt I had to do was watch over John's Mom. I had promised John the day he died that I would take care of her just as he would have and I was going to do everything in my power to keep that promise.

I called Mom every day, most days more than once. The first couple of weeks she seemed all right and she tried very hard to keep my spirits up. She was very focused on updating her will and trust papers. Ironically, she had formed the trust just that year, naming John as her beneficiary and power of attorney with me as back-up. Now, she had to change that. How hard it must be for a mother to outlive yet another child. Poor Frances. But the paperwork seemed to give her a sense of purpose for which I was grateful. However, as soon as that task was done, she immediately started to go downhill. Frances finally admitted to me that she had started falling at home. I was so afraid she would get seriously hurt and I was frustrated being so far away. In my own compromised state, I was in no shape to travel to Texas and care for her. I enlisted the assistance of her neighbor and convinced Frances to be seen by her doctor. He immediately hospitalized her for a complete work-up. The doctors, however, could find nothing medically wrong beyond aging. Yet, none of us felt she could live alone any more. I wanted her here with me so I could make sure all was well. She agreed.

So, I decided to have her flown out to Arizona and settled her in a beautiful assisted living home in Scottsdale.

And through it all, I felt I was being watched over. Certainly by God, but also by John.

There were coincidences that were so striking that I was sure they were not just random occurrences.

It seemed as if John's soul knew what was coming. Home projects he had put off or dragged on suddenly were finished right before he passed. John had passed away at the end of our trip – a weekend full of family, love, and laughter. He even chose to die at a hotel far from home so that our house would never be saddened or tainted by the memory of him leaving. And he chose to go in the middle of the night when I was asleep. It's usually hard for me to sleep in a strange bed but I remember to this day thinking that it was unusual that I felt so tired that last night and I still remember drifting off right away. When I awoke, John was long gone. I had been spared having to witness his departure, something I know would have destroyed me.

And then there was the practical. Right after I returned home I knew I had to evaluate our finances. Luckily, I had elected to take early Social Security which had just started. But I was going to lose John's Social Security check as well as his income from his job as a nurse. And then there was the issue of health insurance. Because I was self-employed, I was carried on John's health insurance policy from his job at HealthSouth Rehab, something that was going to go away within days of his passing. I had only turned sixty-two a couple of months prior. Sixty-five and Medicare was a long way off. So I got on the Internet to investigate COBRA. It was my understanding that I only would be able to use that for eighteen months. That would still leave a large expensive gap. Then what? There again, John had carefully calculated. As it turned out, when health insurance is lost because of the death of a spouse, COBRA is available for three years! That would safely put me on Medicare before the insurance ran out.

All of this helped me to believe that I was not alone in this devastating journey.

But was that so?

Or was this just wishful thinking brought on by my overwhelming grief?

I had to know.

I continued researching, looking for that definitive lecture on Heaven.

Then a life-changing synchronicity occurred.

Chapter Eleven

C8

A few weeks after John had passed, I received an email from a fellow nurse named Amanda. She and I had worked together as Case Managers at Tri-West years before and we had kept in touch off and on. But life and circumstances had gotten in the way and we hadn't communicated in a few years. Yet, here she was. Her email caught my attention. She told me that she had had a dream about me the night before and felt compelled to contact me. She had heard about my loss a few weeks prior but had lost my email address. Then, spurred on by her dream, she had just that morning requested my email address from a mutual friend. Amanda told me she had recently lost her brother-in-law and had found a particular book very comforting.

The book was *Soul Shift: Finding Where the Dead Go* by Mark Ireland. Mark was a businessman whose late father, Richard Ireland, was a minister and renowned psychic and medium during the 1960's. However, Mark had followed a more conventional

Joy Collins

career path until the sudden death of his youngest son in 2004. Like me, Mark had had an overwhelming need to know what had happened to his son after he left this earth and wanted to communicate with him. The book told Mark's story from his point of view – how he found mediums who communicated with his son's spirit and who helped Mark heal. The book also recounted Mark's own spiritual and psychic journey.

Amanda had read the book and found it both reassuring and uplifting. She thought I would too and urged me to read it. I was hungry for anything that would help my deep sorrow so I immediately bought the book.

Amanda was 100% right. I felt an immediate kinship with Mark. The feelings he described mirrored my own. The need he had for reassurance resonated with me. He was even a fellow Arizonan. I devoured the book within days. It helped but it also left me wanting more. I logged on to my computer and searched for more books like this one. Here finally was what I was searching for. No more platitudes about discarding clothing and removing rings. No talk about "moving on". Here was nuts and bolts stuff about the afterlife, what it was like for me and what it might be like for John. And, finally, here was confirmation that these inklings and feelings I was having that John was not only still with me but communicating with me were real and not my imagination.

Mark talked about readings he had had with mediums and for the first time I contemplated the idea for myself. I had been a fan of the television series "Medium" but never considered engaging a medium on my own. Yet, I firmly believed some people had this gift and I wondered what was out there. What could they tell me that would help me? I researched well known mediums and found many had written books about their lives and experiences. I quickly ordered a bunch of them. Before long the floor next to my bed was littered with books by George Anderson, Alison Dubois, Carole Obley, and others. Eventually I had so many books I needed to buy an extra bookcase just to hold them all. Soon I needed a second one. The mound of books grew and finally a sliver of peace started to peek its head above the sea of despair that I was drowning in.

Maybe it was the reassurances I was getting from my new-found metaphysical books or maybe it was just time but it seemed to me that John was now communicating with me more and more.

It started with dreams. I learned from my reading that the very vivid dream I had had of John coming back to say good-bye the first night after he passed was actually a visit. One of the things I regretted most was that John left suddenly and I didn't have the opportunity to let him know one last time how much I loved him and we didn't get a chance to say good-bye. Now I knew that we did. We had our good-bye after all.

Then, my cousin Claudia told me that she had a dream that was very real as well. In it, John consoled her when she was crying because he had died. John hugged her and told her it was his time to go. She said when she woke up she felt comforted and that his hug had felt very real.

Then that summer I started having many dreams. Most of them were just dreams, silly and disjointed as dreams usually are. Regardless, I was glad to have them because even for a few brief albeit sometimes illogical seconds, I was with John again. But a few of the dreams were very real and memorable. Some just lasted for a few moments but the feeling of comfort lasted after I woke up. Two are still very much with me even after all these years.

In one dream, John and I were in a place that resembled a bar. It was well-lit and very upscale, more like the kind of bar you find at the front of a very nice restaurant. I can't remember now who else was with us but I had the impression that there were friends all around us and the atmosphere was very happy. John's energy was very high and he was smiling broadly (this dream was over four years ago and I still remember details – another sign that this was a visitation). Anyway, John had to go off to a meeting but before he left he held me tightly and we told each other "I love you". John said that he was back now and he would never leave me again. He told me that he would be right back and then we were going to go home together. I remember I was very happy to be with him and I felt him touch and hold me.

But this is the dream that blew my mind.

Here is the back story: Many of the staff from John's last job at HealthSouth Rehab Hospital came to his viewing at the funeral home. I vaguely remember meeting them. I remember lots of tears. John was well-loved at his job. I do remember the Human Resources person greeting me and telling me I needed to take care of the insurance issues. I remember thinking how odd she would bring that up when I was standing next to my husband's casket. Frankly, it struck me as rude and callous. I also remember asking her if John had anything at work that I needed to pick up. Did he have a locker? She told me No to both questions.

Based on that information I didn't give it another thought. I had plenty of other things to think about. After the funeral, I went through John's effects, particularly his wallet. I didn't know what I was looking for. Nothing in particular. I just liked touching things he had touched. He kept some small denomination bills in a side pocket of his wallet. He called it his "tip stash", a way of keeping small bills that he could use to tip people. I took those bills and put them in a side pocket in my wallet so I would have something of his to carry with me. There were also business cards. One had writing on the back, three numbers separated by hyphens. Again, I just filed the information in the back of my mind and put the wallet in a box I was using to keep all his keepsakes.

Three and half months later, I had what was probably one of the most vivid dreams of John I have ever had. In it John and I were together in a building that resembled a church because it had pews. It also resembled a courtroom or a place like that because people were speaking at the front of the room. John was wearing a very white and vibrant shirt that almost seemed to glow. Then he told me he had to leave. I reached for his hand but he got away from me and I lost him in a crowd that was heading out the door at the back of this large room. Beyond the door was a very bright light that shone over everything. All the people who had been visiting with loved ones left through that door. I called John's name but he was gone.

Then I turned to someone who was with me (I don't know who this person was). I was crying but I told her "But it was a good visit." So, on some level I knew that John was dead.

Then I looked down on the pew where I had put my purse and John's backpack was there next it. He had left it behind. I remember touching it and feeling it and squeezing it and realizing it was empty except for some papers inside it.

Then I woke up. In that instant, I realized I never got John's brown leather backpack from work. He carried that backpack every day. It was four o'clock in the morning but I suddenly had the need to have that backpack NOW. Maybe it was in John's car. How could I have forgotten about it?

John's car was in our driveway. I grabbed my keys and a flashlight and headed out to the driveway. I looked everywhere in that car – under all the seats, in the trunk. The backpack was nowhere to be found. I went back into the house devastated.

Then it hit me – the card with the numbers written on the back. That was it! That was a combination to a lock. Despite what the Human Resources manager had told me, could it be that John really did have a locker at work and the backpack was there?

It was too early to call the hospital to find out. I would somehow have to make it through the next three hours. I prayed to John to help me and fell back to sleep.

At seven o'clock when I knew the Head Nurse would be in I called the nursing station. She remembered me and was very kind. Through tears I told her why I was calling.

"Can you please check for me? I think John might have a locker there. If he does, I need to have his things."

"Hang on a minute and let me check."

Within minutes she was back and from the sound of her voice I could tell that she was both amazed and happy to relay the information. "Joy, you're right. He does have a locker here and it has a padlock on it."

"I think I have the combination to it." I gave her the numbers written on the back of the business card.

"Joy, we'll try that number. But, believe me, if those numbers don't work, I will get Maintenance here to break in. I'll get that locker open for you. Give me a few minutes and I'll call you right back."

It seemed like forever but she called me back within ten minutes. "Joy - that was the combination. We got in. I have John's things here. I'll pack them up for you and you can come down to pick them up whenever you want."

"Can you tell me what was in there?"

"Just some personal items his backpack, his stethoscope and some little things."

I couldn't believe my ears. John had told me how to get his backpack. If I hadn't seen and picked up that backpack in my dream, I would have forgotten all about it. But John wouldn't let me forget. He knew what it meant to me – and him. I hugged the backpack when I got it back. There was nothing earth-shattering in it. No big stash of money or anything like that. But it did contain things that meant a lot to John and thus a lot to me – his stethoscope, his work watch (that I had given him), a packet of photos of me and the furbabies, his gold chain that he often wore around his neck. John things. Love things.

There were other "signs" (these are in no special order but happened in the first few months after John passed):

➢ One Saturday a friend insisted on taking me to breakfast. She picked me up in her van and we drove to Mimi's in Scottsdale. We were meeting two other friends there. We pulled into the parking lot and she parked away from the other cars next to a small island with a cement curb around it. There were several in the large lot, each with a light in it. As soon as she put the car in park, I opened the door and jumped out. The island was on my side. As my feet hit the ground I noticed stenciling on the side of the curb. "Johnny was here". My heart caught. Of all the things to see that morning, why that? Why then? I didn't say anything to my friend but I was spooked.

Days later I drove back there by myself. I needed to look at

100

that again. Imagine my surprise when I found no writing on that curb and no evidence that it had ever been there.

➢　　Claudia told me she had had an experience too. The first night back in the city after she had dropped me off at the airport some friends called her to take her out to dinner. They knew what had happened and didn't want her to be alone. They asked her where she wanted to go. Claudia picked a Mexican restaurant. She later told me her rationale was that since she hated Mexican food she would probably never go back to this restaurant and so would not be forced to associate the sad memory of that day with a restaurant in the future. So, that's where they went. And in the middle of the meal in that Mexican restaurant she heard playing overhead Bob Dylan singing "Lay Lady Lay", a favorite of John's, one he always dedicated to me since our first bed in the apartment I sublet was a big brass bed. Who plays that in a Mexican restaurant? That evening she also felt someone tug on her purse as she crossed a street and when she turned to see who it was no one was there.

➢　　I often experienced heart-wrenching sobbing episodes those first few months after John passed. They would be triggered by anything and nothing and would just take over. I had no recourse other than to see them through. One bout overtook me as I was sitting on our bed. I sobbed as if my insides would come out. It often upset our dogs, Toby especially. This day she jumped on the bed and pushed herself as close as she could to my body. In her doggie way, she was trying to comfort me and make my crying stop. I hugged her but I kept on crying and sobbing. To this day, I know exactly how we were sitting. I was sitting cross-legged on John's side of the bed and Toby was on my left side. I had my left arm around her hind area, pulling her close to me. Suddenly, in the midst of my crying, I felt a sensation on my left hand. It felt as if someone was holding my hand, wrapping their hand around my left hand as if to console me. But except for the animals, I was alone in the house. The touch only lasted a second but it was real. In fact, it was so real that it startled me and I instinctively pulled my hand away before I even could think what it was. All I knew is that at that moment "someone" had physically touched me. My heart told me it had to be John. He saw how much I was hurting and tried to help.

➢   I was grocery shopping in Safeway one afternoon thinking about John and missing him (when didn't I?). Suddenly the theme song from the movie "The Good-bye Girl" came on over the overhead loudspeaker. That movie, and thus that song, had special meaning for me and John. John and I watched it together very early on in our relationship. For those of you not familiar with the story: Richard Dreyfuss and Marsha Mason portray characters who are strangers to each other but are forced to rent an apartment in New York together because of a misunderstanding. She is a divorced single mother and Richard is an actor. He also plays the guitar and that guitar is one of his few prized possessions. Over the course of the movie they become friends and then lovers and Marsha tries very hard to overcome her cynicism about men. Then, in the last few minutes of the movie, Richard gets an out of town acting job and leaves to go on location. Marsha is devastated, convinced he is leaving her like all the other important people in her life. In the last scene, Richard calls her from a pay phone and not only promises to come back to her but asks her to restring his guitar that he had left behind in what is now their apartment. Marsha is ecstatic as she cries out to her daughter "He left his guitar!" Her daughter responds "He IS coming back!" Cue music and credits roll. That movie gets to me every time I watch it.

But in our early years it was also personal. John had a beautiful singing voice and had sung semi-professionally in his youth. He had a Gibson guitar that he loved and cherished and used it when he serenaded me in our courting days. We were dating only a few weeks when he decided to leave his precious guitar at my apartment and I knew then, just like Marsha Mason in that movie, that John was in this for the long haul. He trusted me with his prize, too. So, that theme song became especially important to both us and whenever we heard that song together, we looked at each other and remembered and knew in our hearts how much we meant to each other.

Now, hearing that song in Safeway, at that moment, I knew was John's way of reaching out to me.

➢   Once I smelled flowers in John's office but there were no fresh flowers around anywhere in the whole house.

➢   Other times I would smell John's hair.

➢   While rummaging through the drawer where the checkbooks were kept I found an old plastic button, the kind that are often attached to greeting cards. This one said simply "You Are Loved."

➢   On the evening of our first wedding anniversary after John had passed – our 29th anniversary – August 28, 2010 – I was driving to a restaurant with two friends. I had decided we were going to celebrate that wonderful day and I hoped John would find some way to be with us. It rained on our drive over to the restaurant and then it suddenly stopped and a beautiful rainbow appeared – a double rainbow.

➢   In the early morning hours of August 31, 2010, I went into John's office and his printer was on and making noises after I had turned it off weeks ago. I know the cats might have done that but maybe John had a hand in that, too.

➢   A friend of mine was a shiatsu practitioner (shiatsu is a Japanese form of bodywork – it's best described as finger pressure massage) and I started having sessions with her after John passed to help ease my stress. I would often have strange sensations during these sessions. Once I had a flash of a vision – John and I were together in a tent in the Old West and he was wearing a buckskin shirt. Months later I was visiting a museum in Phoenix and saw that exact same shirt in a Western exhibit.

➢   During another shiatsu treatment, I had another strange and remarkable experience. I felt John loving me. He was happy and wanted me to be happy. At the end of the treatment, with my eyes closed, I saw myself being enveloped in a white light that turned into the most beautiful blue color and I just wanted to go into it. I wondered if that was where John was and if that was what it was like for him.

These were just some of the things that were happening and

103

Joy Collins

catching my attention but I still wondered if these occurrences were just my imagination. Were they being manufactured by my broken heart? I needed and wanted more. I kept journaling and talking to John. I prayed. I knew if there was an answer out there it would come.

And it did – in a very big way.

Chapter Twelve
CB

     Amanda and I had been keeping in touch via email and that fall she asked me if I wanted to accompany her to see one of the mediums I had read about in Mark Ireland's book. The medium was Jamie Clark and he was doing a group reading at a metaphysical book store in Scottsdale called "A Peace of the Universe". I immediately agreed to go. Jamie was a local medium but known nationally and well respected. I admit I was apprehensive but if this meant I would be able to connect with John, I was willing to put aside my anxiety.

     I prepared myself the day of the reading as if I were going on a date. The group reading was scheduled for seven in the evening, right after the shop had closed. I dressed and primped. I was nervous. I put John's wedding ring on a ribbon around my neck. I felt good holding that part of him close to me but I also hoped that energy would help with the reading. I spoke to John and told him it was okay if he didn't come through. I had no idea how he felt about this.

What if this wasn't what he wanted me to do? But then I figured if it wasn't, he wouldn't have led me to this opportunity. Maybe this was his way of helping me. Maybe he wanted to connect with me as much as I wanted to connect with him. Based on my dreams and other signs that I was now starting to recognize, I knew John was still with me.

I played a CD in my car as I drove over to meet Amanda in Scottsdale and it seemed that the songs I picked were sending me messages from John. In the lyrics of the song "Just Around the Corner" I felt that John was truly telling me how close he was to me all the time. Was this his way of letting me know that he was going to come through in the reading? I had no idea. I didn't know if I should wish for it to happen or not. If he didn't I would be disappointed. If he did, what would I find out and how would I know it was him?

I arrived at the shop before Amanda and paid my fee. Others were already in attendance and the energy level was high. About twenty chairs had been arranged in a circle at the back of the shop. I paced around the room and was happy to see Amanda arrive about ten minutes later. After she paid her fee we took our seats. Amanda sat to my left. I had no idea what to expect but everyone there seemed about as excited and nervous as I did so I didn't feel alone.

At seven sharp, Jamie entered the room from the rear of the shop. He was a short good-looking man and I could sense his energy. He smiled a lot and seemed genuinely happy to be doing what he did. He introduced himself and gave a brief description of what he was about to do. He explained he had no control over who would come through but he said that it was all good and our loved ones wanted to communicate with us as much as we wanted to hear from them. He handed out pieces of paper so that we could take notes when he started receiving information. As it turned out, we all spontaneously began writing for each other as the readings progressed because it was impossible to listen and write at the same time when the reading was our own.

Then Jaimie said a short prayer thanking God and asking for

protection. He took a deep breath and started.

He immediately zeroed in on a woman four seats to my left. She was older and was with three younger women who appeared to be in their teens or early twenties. Jaimie spent a few minutes with her giving her quite a bit of information that seemed to touch all of them. Then he took another breath and started slowly walking down the line. He stopped as soon as he reached me and looked right at me. My heart started beating very fast.

"I am feeling a male energy same level as you. I am hesitant to say this but has your husband passed?"

I swallowed hard. "Yes."

Jamie continued. "He comes in very powerfully. He sits very casually, very relaxed." Jamie imitated someone sitting back casually on a chair and I smiled. That was John.

Jamie continued. "He is known for his eyes." (The first thing I ever remember noticing about John was his eyes. They looked right at me and made me feel so special.) "He thanks you for being a caretaker. You always understood him for who he was. He was a great man, different. He loves you very much. You addressed things and he appreciated that. (John always told me how he loved that I took charge and got things done – when we suspected he had prostate surgery, when he needed a pacemaker.)

Then Jamie came through with a name "a D name". David was John's younger brother who had pre-deceased him by nine years. "This person and another person who left quickly came for him." (This might have been John's father who had passed suddenly in 2008.) Jaimie then grabbed his chest. "Quick – he was done. Like a heart attack. They came for your husband. He's okay. He shows himself to me as if he is dancing."

Jamie mentioned a few other things in quick succession. He confirmed John's father. He mentioned someone else who might have been John's aunt who was also deceased. He picked up the energy of a young soul – possibly a miscarriage I had had.

Jamie stopped and concentrated for a few seconds before going on. "I get a feeling of tingling in the left hip." I had recently developed a shingles rash and it was affecting my left sciatic nerve. I acknowledged understanding this reference. "He says to take care of yourself. Be open to treatment. He's very positive about this. Take whatever is offered to you. It will help you."

And then it was over. Repeating the words here doesn't give the experience justice. What Jamie said might not mean all that much to anyone else but to me they were words straight from Heaven and straight from John. He said things in a way that I truly felt he was hearing John and John was speaking to me through him. I felt a sense of peace and I was so grateful.

Then Jamie moved on down the row and started reading for another woman.

I looked at Amanda, tears welling in my eyes. I had felt John while Jamie was talking. I just knew in my heart that it had been real, not just my imagination and not just lucky guesses on Jamie's part. Those around me handed me the sheets of paper they had been writing on, recording for me what Jamie had said. Those papers became my lifeline to John. What was once just paper was now precious words from John. He was alive, he was okay, he still loved me. I can't describe how good I felt, how happy.

I listened intently as Jamie went around the circle and read for others. Tears flowed and hearts were healed. The energy in the room felt so good.

The readings went on for about an hour and then Jamie stopped. He thanked everyone, smiled that infectious smile and left the way he had come.

I was overwhelmed. I had wanted so much to hear from John and now it had happened.

Amanda and I went out for coffee afterwards and talked about what we had just experienced. Her late brother-in-law had also come through in the session and we were both overcome.

I don't remember driving home that night. All I know is that I was happy beyond words. John was okay. He was alive and well. He still loved me.

And more importantly, he was still John, my John.

Chapter Thirteen

CB

The euphoria of feeling John so close to me wore off soon, however, as life once again intruded. Despite the drain my grief took on me, I still had obligations that I was not going to ignore. John's Mom was still in the assisted living home and needed me to be her advocate and watch over her care. Her cat Friskie was still living with me. And Friskie was not acclimating well to my household. It was becoming apparent I was going to have to make other arrangements soon.

And I was still reeling from losing our cat Charlotte. The day before I flew John's Mom out to Arizona along with Friskie, I had had to put Charlotte down.

Charlotte's story:

Charlotte was a very special kitty. She was described as a "diluted" calico by the shelter. I have no idea what they meant by that. All I knew was that Charlotte was a beautiful long-haired cat.

She was only six weeks old when I brought her home. John and I had recently lost two of the three cats we had brought out to Arizona due to old age. We were now down to one very old ginger cat named Smudge.

In March 1995, I had gone to a job interview in Phoenix and made the mistake of stopping at the Arizona Humane Society on Hatcher Road on the way back home. I called John on my cell phone from what was called "the kitten room". It was a room full of six-week-old kittens, all cute, all running around just waiting to sucker in someone like me.

"Guess where I am?" I asked John.

He knew from the sound of my voice where I was. We had talked about adoption recently and he knew we were in deep trouble.

"Pick out two and come home" was all he said.

I had already picked out a beautiful little calico and turned around to see who else might be good for our home. I had placed my purse on the floor while I looked and now turned around to find that a little white furball with pale patches of gray and brown was trying to crawl into it. I had been chosen. Charlotte had decided she was going home with me.

Ever the writer, when it came time to naming the two new babies, I wanted to go with Emily and Charlotte after the Bronte sisters. But the calico was a tomboy and Emily didn't suit her so John named her Casey after a cat he had had when he was younger. But Charlotte's name fit her. I later found out it meant "little woman" and that is exactly what she was. She was always a sweet little girl who loved to snuggle. She had an endearing way of putting her little paw on a person's cheek and just lightly tapping it. John loved to cuddle with her listening to what he called her "gentle purrs". He had many nicknames for her, among them "little Charlotta" and "crankypants" because she had lots to say when she wanted something.

But our little Charlotta became very ill a few weeks before John passed. We had blood work drawn and an ultrasound of her abdomen done. The verdict was either colitis or lymphoma. The first was not good but livable. The second was probably a death sentence. The treatment was the same for both – medication – so we opted to just do that and keep her comfortable. We refused the biopsy. We did not want to put her through any more. She would be loved and cherished for as long as she chose to stay with us.

The day of John's funeral it was obvious that Charlotte was much worse. She woke me up during the night (not that I was sleeping much anyway) with vomiting and was in obvious distress. My vets got me through the next few days as well as they could. Medication and fluids kept her comfortable. A couple of weeks later, my friend Shelley who was very metaphysical visited and she "spoke" with Charlotte. She told me that Charlotte promised to hang in with me if she could. She knew I wasn't ready to let her go so soon after John. Little Charlotte knew I needed her.

Charlotte kept her word for two more months. With medication and IV therapy we kept her comfortable but on August 4, 2010, just ten weeks after John had passed, I held Charlotte in my arms for the last time as she crossed over too. I envisioned John waiting for her and it helped a little to think of them together again.

I mourned the loss of our sweet baby but life quickly took over. The next day Mom arrived via air ambulance along with her cat Friskie. I had Mom admitted to HealthSouth Rehab where John had worked. She needed a complete workup to see exactly what was wrong. She had quickly deteriorated after John had passed. She went from total independence to falling at home and unable to care for herself within three weeks. She had been admitted to a hospital in her home town in Texas but after a couple of weeks her doctors could find nothing specifically wrong. She continued to deteriorate though so she had been transferred to a local nursing home. Within a couple of weeks, she became totally incoherent. The nursing home staff claimed she was doing well but I was becoming concerned. I called her every day and I could tell she was becoming less and less alert. I was upset to have her so far away from me.

Then everything came to a head in mid-July. Mom's neighbor from across the street was my lifeline. This sweet angel visited Mom in the nursing home while she also kept an eye on her house and fed her cat. One evening in July after Mom had been at the nursing home about three weeks, Karen called me at home, upset.

"Joy, I went to visit Frances tonight and I'm really worried about her. They are not treating her well."

I trusted Karen's judgment and asked her to explain to me what was going on. She told me that when she went to visit Frances that evening she found her with her nightgown pulled up to her neck (this was not how modest Frances would be at all!) and lying sideways in her bed. She said Mom was soaking in urine and had no idea where or who she was. I was livid. This was the last straw. The nursing staff had been repeatedly telling me that all was well every time I had asked for a report but this was obviously not the case.

I thanked Karen for telling me and reassured her that I would take care of this immediately.

As soon as I hung up with Karen, I called the nursing station and asked to speak to Mom's nurse. She feigned ignorance of the situation and tried to tell me that things must have just deteriorated recently. My nursing instincts told me this was not the case at all and I told her so.

"Read me every single medication you have her on," I demanded. The nurse did. Mom was on thirteen different medications and half of them were sedating! No wonder she was so confused. I rattled off which ones I wanted discontinued immediately. The nurse tried to object.

"Don't give me an argument. You call her doctor right now and get this taken care of. And have the nursing supervisor call me within the hour."

I had gone into protective mode. I think all the weeks of frustration and anger and feeling so helpless after John had passed finally coalesced around Mom's need for an advocate. I could protect her and make sure she received the care she needed. It was also painfully clear that she needed to be in Arizona with me – now! – so that I could keep an eye on her.

When the nursing supervisor called me I let loose.

"I'm so sorry that this has happened. Please be assured that we are doing everything we can to make sure your mother-in-law is being well cared for," she said.

I knew exactly what she was doing and I was having none of it. I was not going to be placated with her recital of the "how to handle the irate family member" guidelines. I told her exactly what I thought of how they were caring for her and over-sedating her so that she would not be a "bother". I informed her that if anything happened to my mother-in-law – anything! – I would welcome the chance to sue them.

"I don't know if my mother-in-law told you what I do for a living but I am a legal nurse consultant. I have lawyers on speed dial and I would love nothing better than to sue the pants off you and your organization."

I was turning into every family member I had ever hated to work with but I no longer cared. Here finally was something I could do. I could protect John's mother and damn it! I was going to do everything possible to see that she was safe and got the best of everything. She deserved that much and I had promised John.

That Monday I started planning to fly Frances out to Arizona so that I could oversee her care. It took two more weeks to get a medical flight set up and her hospital transfer arranged. I wanted her medically evaluated as soon as she arrived. I had no idea what was wrong and I no longer trusted any of her doctors. HealthSouth Rehab Hospital agreed to take her and do a complete workup as well as devise a plan to get her as strong as possible. In the meantime, I started looking for an assisted living home that Mom could transfer to once she was strong enough. And as I mentioned before, Mom's cat Friskie was coming with her. The idea was for Friskie to become another cat in my household. I just hoped it would work out.

The timing was eerie. Those last few weeks before Mom arrived Charlotte kept getting worse and worse. She was rapidly failing and I knew she didn't have long. Every time it was close, my vet would ask if I was ready and my answer was always "No".

Joy Collins

But now I knew I had to think of Charlotte and not myself.
She was tired. She needed to rest. The fluids and medication were
no longer working. She wasn't eating and her little body was ready
to go. I knew John was waiting for her. He would take care of our
Crankypants.

So, in the early evening hours of August 4, 2010 Dr. Tom
came to the house and while I held Charlotte one last time, he helped
her over the Rainbow Bridge. I cried so hard. My heart was broken.
Another loss.

Then the next day Mom and Friskie arrived and I welcomed
the distraction. Mom did very well in the hospital. Although her
overall health was no longer good her mental state cleared once
many of the sedating medications were out of her system. She
regained some strength and could use a walker. After two weeks,
she transitioned to a lovely assisted living home in Scottsdale. She
was now only a fifteen-minute drive from my home and I felt better
having her closer to me.

Friskie did not fare as well. She had been an only cat when
she lived with Mom. Now she had three new cat siblings and two
dog siblings and she was terrified. I kept her separated from the other
animals and hoped and prayed that over time she would settle down
and accept her new life.

She didn't. Days turned into weeks and weeks into months
and still I was playing musical rooms and animals.

One night in November, just a few weeks after my reading
from Jaimie, I was watching videos alone in the bedroom with the
door closed so that Friskie could be with me with no interruptions.
She slept next to me on the bed which was nice. Suddenly there was
the distinct sound of a cat jumping down onto the floor to my left
and I saw a fleeting shadow of a cat. I knew it wasn't Friskie. She
was still sleeping next to me. Then that night Charlotte "visited" me
in a dream. She was healthy and chubby just like she used to be in
the old days and she rubbed against me and let me pet her. And in
the dream, I knew she was dead. When I woke up, I was ecstatic.
My Charlotta had visited me and she told me that she was okay and

114

happy.

A couple of weeks later a friend of mine agreed to take Friskie into her home. Friskie was once again an only animal and she was happy too. Maybe Charlotte helped me with that as well.

Regardless, it was becoming more and more obvious to me that there was a lot more to this metaphysical stuff and I was anxious to learn more.

Chapter Fourteen

CB

After my reading with Jamie I was even more intent on reading everything I could get my hands on that even had a whiff of the metaphysical and the afterlife. The more I learned, the more I wanted to learn. I was quickly becoming obsessed. But I didn't care.

Finally, I was getting satisfaction.

Finally, I was finding people who could help me make some sense of what I was going through.

Finally, I was getting the real "lecture on heaven" that John had always teased me about. I wonder if on some level he knew.

I started a blog in addition to the journal I was already keeping. I didn't care if anyone read it but I felt the need to memorialize what I was going through. If it helped others who were in the same boat as I was, so much the better.

I knew in my heart of hearts there had to be a reason why I was still here. Right after John passed I was hoping I would pass, too. I had read so many stories of couples who were closely bonded who died within weeks of each other. I knew there truly was such a thing as "broken heart syndrome" and I hoped I had it. I couldn't face the prospect of being here without John. It was awful and terrifying. The flashbacks were subsiding somewhat but I still had them. I knew I was going to have to do something about them if they didn't start to diminish soon.

And another fresh hell was soon to start – the holidays were fast approaching. I dreaded them so much. I knew the only way I was going to get through them was to ignore them. At least, in my own world.

And luckily, I had my mother-in-law's care to distract me. While she was doing well in the assisted living home, Frances still needed me to oversee her care. She was mentally very alert but physically weaker. It was hard for her to use the walker now and it was obvious that she had reached a new level of dependence. She now qualified for Hospice. I knew soon I would be facing another loss but I hoped it was not for a while. I wasn't ready. I visited her three times a week and we enjoyed our time together. It warmed my heart to see the smile on her face when I walked into the room and she knew it was me. My relationship with my own mother had been strained for most of my adult life and recently had taken a turn for the worst. Frances gave me the gift of being someone's daughter in a way I never had before and I loved her for it. Plus, she was my link to John. Frances told me stories about John from his childhood. She talked about her days when she was first married. I needn't have worried how we were going to pass the time. Frances was as glad to see me as I was to see her.

In addition to monitoring Frances' physical care, I was also now in charge of managing her finances, which, in addition to paying her bills, also included overseeing the maintenance of her house in Texas. I discussed its disposition with her and she agreed selling it was the best thing to do. We both knew she was never going back there. But easier said than done as the house was still exactly how she had left it at the end of June when she was first admitted to the hospital. Karen, her neighbor, had continued to look in on it from time to time but it was now incumbent upon me to get it emptied out and ready for sale. This meant traveling to Texas and going through all her belongings, room by room, drawer by drawer. I needed to decide what to keep, what to toss, and what to donate. How was I going to do this when I could barely get through a day in my own home? I was still feeling very overwhelmed with just the ordinary day to day living. Now this new task seemed insurmountable. Mercifully, I had my friend Louise who volunteered to go with me for a few days. I hated traveling alone anyway and I knew this trip was going to be difficult on so many levels. We planned the trip for the first week in November so that it wouldn't interfere with anyone's holiday plans. Just because I had chosen to ignore them didn't mean that everyone else was.

I also finally made an appointment to have my first session with a therapist for the week after I came back. I knew I was going to need it. Things were not getting any easier.

Somehow I got through the trip to Texas. Louise was a big help. Cleaning out the house was a major undertaking, both physically and emotionally. I felt a responsibility to keep things. It was so depressing to know that there was essentially no family left, that I was now the keeper of the memories. Frances was the last of her family. Her brothers and sisters were dead and of course her parents. Her husband was gone and now both of her children. Her younger son had no wife or children so there was no one left from that lineage. John had three children but they were estranged from all of us. The only relatives were some nieces and nephews from Frances' husband's side of the family but they weren't close and I didn't know them. I was it! Where to start? What was important to keep and why? After I was gone, who was going to care?

In addition to disposing of what was in the house, I had arranged to meet with her financial advisor. I was not surprised to learn that Frances and her husband had done very well saving what they had earned over the years. I had often teased John that there was money there and he was going to inherit a small fortune. He never believed me. But I was right and I was very happy to learn

119

that I had more than enough funds to care for Frances. I was determined that she was going to get the very best of care. It was the least I could do for her.

In just four days, Louise and I went through the house as best we could and packed up what I thought we should save. In addition to clothes for Frances I salvaged family pictures and home movies. I also signed a contract with a local real estate agent. She was going to put the house on the market as well as help me get rid of the furniture that was left there.

Then Louise and I headed back home. It was time to face the holidays, my first without John.

Chapter Fifteen

CB

I continued my metaphysical quest which was fast becoming an obsession. But I didn't care. If it was an addiction, who was it hurting? At least it gave me something to do and distracted me from being depressed.

I had my first appointment with my therapist the week after I returned from Texas. Carolyn was a soft-spoken and kind woman. But she knew her stuff. She validated the emotions that I was feeling and gave me the space I needed to grieve. I didn't hear one platitude about moving on and I liked her immediately. She also appeared to have the same beliefs I did regarding the metaphysical so I was free to share my feelings about continuing my contact with John. All in all, she felt I was doing well considering the circumstances. I wasn't sure I agreed with her. It was still hard for me to talk about losing John with her without crying. But she was the expert so I had to believe her when she said I was all right. We agreed to meet at least every other week in the short term and then take it from there. She also thought some EMDR therapy would help with the flashbacks I was still experiencing. EMDR stands for Eye Movement Desensitization and Reprocessing. It includes rapid eye movement and is a form of psychotherapy that is used primarily to treat PTSD.

I also decided to bend a little with my plan to ignore the holidays. I wasn't going to decorate the house or put up a tree. I couldn't bear to open the boxes that contained the ornaments that John and I had gathered over the years or see our stockings with everyone's names, especially John's and Charlotte's. But I decided I would shop for presents for my family and friends. Nothing big. Just some little things to show them that I still cared and was thinking about them.

One of the women I was going to shop for was my friend Sherri. One of her passions was angels and I decided to get her something with an angel theme for Christmas. The evening after my first therapy session I headed out to Scottsdale to once again visit A Peace of the Universe, the same new age shop where Jaimie had done his reading a few weeks before. I had no idea what I was going to get. I just trusted it would show itself to me.

As soon as I entered the shop I was greeted by the owner, a woman who has smiled every time I have been in her company.

"Hello and welcome," she said. "Can I help you find something?"

"I'm not sure what I am looking for. I'm buying a Christmas present for a friend and she likes angels."

"Well, we have no shortage of them here," and she pointed to an area of the shop where angels were on display in a corner curio cabinet.

I thanked her and headed over to that part of the store. After choosing one that I thought would be just the right angel figurine for Sherri, I decided to look over the other shelves in the store in case something else caught my eye. I had a feeling there was something else there for me but I had no idea what. There were shelves and shelves of books and tarot cards and incense and crystals and all other manner of new age and spiritual items but nothing grabbed me.

Still, I felt I should keep looking.

Finally, I made my way back around to where I had started at the angel display. Next to the angels was a small table with a basket of stones that were glued together in various configurations. Most were in the shape of little angels. I hadn't noticed them before when I was shopping for Sherri. Now, however, I felt compelled to go through them and I also had the urge to buy one for myself. I dug my hand into the basket and pulled one out.

My heart nearly stopped when I looked at what I was holding. It was a small stone angel and written across it was "I Will Never Leave You". Immediately I felt John with me and knew he had wanted me to have this. It was his message to me.

I smiled and happily purchased both items. When I got home, I glued the little stone angel with its comforting message to the framed picture of John that I had placed on my nightstand. It would be a daily reminder to me from him that we were indeed doing this together. It wasn't my imagination. John was with me. He would always be with me.

PART THREE

TEACH

How we can continue our relationship with our soul mates

Chapter Sixteen

ભ

While writing this book, I wondered how best to express the journey I have been on. I didn't want to bore you with a mundane chronology of facts. I wanted to help you understand what it has meant to me to learn the things that I have learned and to experience what it was like for me to lose my soul mate in this life. And how I continue to move forward.

Notice I didn't say move on. I hate that phrase. "Move on." To me it meant leaving John behind and I have no intention of doing that. No, I am going forward and I am bringing him with me. He and I are going through this next phase of our relationship *together*. That has been something I knew in my heart to be true from the very first day. I remember having that thought in the hotel room as I waited for the hotel clerk to come to my room after I had cried over the phone. Yes, I was miserable and devastated at losing John. Yes, I was in shock. But a part of my heart knew he was still with me and we would continue our relationship together. I didn't know how at that time. It was just a feeling. But I believed in us, I trusted John and his love for me – for us - and I knew if there was a way, we would find it.

It is my personal belief that losing a soul mate is truly a very difficult event. I am assuming you are reading this book because you, too, have lost your soul mate. There are hundreds of books out there addressing grief. Believe me, I read many of them. Most addressed grief in general terms and sorely lacked what I needed. Especially because none, I felt, addressed the particular loss of a mate who was a soul mate, or as some refer to it, a Twin Flame. I am not belittling anyone's experience of losing a loved one to death. Every loss is hard in its own unique way. But married soul mates are bonded in a way like no other. When that physical bond is separated by death, it is devastating in a way that is extremely hard. I have already expressed some of why I believe that to be true, but I will delve into that further in a little bit.

But even having said that, do I know how you feel?

No, I do not.

My feelings, my personal experiences, are completely different from yours.

The exact same gut-wrenching moment visited each of us — but it is, in no way, exact.

Or comparable.

Or shared.

That pain is in the deepest core of each of us. The place we didn't know we had.

Until it happened.

And we saw.

And felt.

And collapsed under its weight.

So, where do I, we, go from here?

Is there a tomorrow? The short answer is Yes.

Right now, in this moment, maybe you don't know if you can face another tomorrow.

I didn't. But John showed me the way.

And together, we can show you.
So, let's start.

Chapter Seventeen

CB

I find that for me to understand something or learn something new, I need to understand the foundations first. So, that is what I am going to do now.

I will start with the basics of soul mate (as I believe and understand it) and the physiology of grief and how they are not only intertwined but that they make our grief different. Not more important, just different. As I mentioned in the Introduction, this is not a contest. All grief is difficult and something I wish none of us had to go through. But soul mate loss has (in my opinion) a unique set of characteristics.

So, let's start with some basic premises.

What is a soul mate?

I think Richard Bach (author of *Jonathan Livingston Seagull*) described it perfectly: "*Our soulmate is the one who makes life come to life.*"

"Life come to life". I love that. John made living so much

Joy Collins

fun. We often said that to each other "I love our life." And we'd smile. It was true.

Our soul mate is the embodiment of "home". I know no other way to describe it. I often said John and I were really Johnandjoy – no spaces between the words. Not that we smothered each other. No, we each had our likes and dislikes, our hobbies and our jobs. We respected each other's space. I could be in my office working while John was in the garage refurbishing an antique car part and life was perfect, knowing the other was there. We knew in the very deepest part of our hearts that we had each other's back, that we could count on each other. In our heyday, John and I were both nurses and worked two double shifts every weekend (traveling by car together two and a half hours each way to get to the job), at the same hospital, most times on the same unit. Then we spent the rest of the week home together, working on the house, or vacationing, or just playing at home. People asked us many times how we did it. Didn't we get tired of each other? The simple answer was No. In fact, even years later, we were often mistaken for newlyweds by people who didn't know us.

Did we have a special secret? I don't know. We had a secret but it wasn't special. You probably have it too if you were lucky enough to be married to your soul mate. Being married to your soul mate is the most loving place in the world to be. Your soul mate both complements and challenges you. By having their faith and confidence, you are encouraged to be the best *you* you can be. I started my own legal nurse consulting business at the age of fifty-four. This meant I quit my full-time job with its benefits and jumped off the cliff into the unknown. But John was behind me 100%, telling me he knew not only that I could do this but that I would be very successful. And I was. That business lasted ten years until I retired.

And it was a two-way street. When John was ill in the hospital awaiting a pacemaker and the doctors were dragging their feet, placing him in danger, I was the one who raised hell and got results. John called me at 5:30 in the morning from his hospital room after spending a horrible night and I could tell just from the sound of his voice that he was worried. Within forty-five minutes I was at his bedside and causing trouble. John knew I was in his corner. He knew all he had to say was he needed my help and it was his. It was faith, pure and simple. No doubts. Not for a minute.

We were home to each other, our soft place to land.

What do I mean by that? Let me try to illustrate.

Do they still foam runways when planes are coming in for a landing and they are in trouble? I remember many years ago - when I was young and enjoyed flying and didn't worry about all the things that could go wrong - being on a plane that was getting ready to land and the pilot was having trouble getting the gear to come down. This probably happened around forty years ago so you must excuse me if the details are a little foggy. All I remember now is that we were told the wheels would not descend properly and we were going to make a risky landing. But the crew on the ground was going to foam the runway for us. I don't remember being scared. We were told what the procedure was going to be and how we needed to respond.

And as it turned out we were far enough out that they had time to play with options.

And all the concern was for naught. Everything ended well. The gear finally came down and we made a safe landing (sans foam) and everyone cheered the pilot for his skill.

But that was what John was for me. He was my layer of runway foam over the world when it grew harsh or stressful. In the past, I would have had John to talk to about anything that was bothering me. To bounce ideas around with. Or to laugh with and, of course, to hug. John was always so good at finding humor in almost anything. In John's embrace, I felt safe and protected.

Since his passing I have missed that and it is only now that I realize just how much I relied on him. I had an inkling before, but I am acutely aware of it now. He was truly my other half, my soul mate, my twin Flame. When the world became too much for me, he was always truly my soft place to land.

Any true separation from each other was intolerable.

133

Joy Collins

And what is more separating than death? The realization that the person who completes you, who is truly your other half is now permanently out of reach is enough to bring you to your knees with grief. I still remember those first few agonizing minutes when I saw John's lifeless body. Disbelief was my first thought – the mind's first instinct is protection and what is better protection than denial? But that can't last very long. Then reality must set in and its enormity is overwhelming. I think back to those first few minutes after finding John when I called our dear friends Louise and Jim back home in Arizona. Louise later told me that she didn't even recognize my voice at first. She said I sounded like a wounded animal. And at that moment of initial intense grief, we are wounded and at our most vulnerable.

And we are experiencing something physical as well as emotional.

Severe profound loss has been linked to something called "broken heart syndrome". You know those stories you have read about married partners dying within days, hours, sometimes even minutes of each other? They are more common than you think. The sudden release of the stress hormones caused by our soul mate's death can temporarily interrupt the pumping heart's normal action. Surviving spouses have sometimes reported the symptoms of a heart attack when, in fact, they did not have a heart attack. But they experienced chest pain and shortness of breath. In some cases, death occurs.

Studies have shown that the surviving spouse has a 66% higher chance of dying in those first few months after a mate's death. People who have lived together for a long time become in sync with each other in more ways than just habits. The heart gives off an electrical charge. How else can it be monitored via EKG or electrocardiogram? Some studies have demonstrated that the heartbeats of lifelong partners may beat in rhythm with each other. When that charge is no longer felt by the remaining heart, disruption occurs.

Is this too "out there" to believe?

Consider this - the shock of grief is real - physically real. When this stress occurs, the hormone cortisol is released by the body. Cortisol is referred to as the "stress hormone". It ramps up your body for protection – for early man, this was to fight off predators. Now you are fighting the predator of grief. So, your heart rate increases, your blood pressure goes up, your nervous system kicks into high gear. No wonder you feel so bad. If this goes on for a long period, as in prolonged intense grief, your body will start to show the effects – disrupted sleep patterns, poor appetite, irritability, fluctuating blood glucose levels, stress on inner organs and blood vessels, even a weakened immune system.

Don't forget, your body has been used to interacting with your mate on the most intimate of levels. You may not have shared the same toothbrush, but you did exchange bodily fluids. His or her germs became yours. For better or worse became true in ways we didn't anticipate on our wedding day.

Our partner's energy projection (their aura, if you will) was also something we interacted with daily. Often, people are not even consciously aware they are intermingling with someone's energy field, yet they perceive it. Haven't you ever entered a room and known instantly that an argument has just taken place between its occupants? On a more personal level, when in the presence of your soul mate, haven't you felt nurtured, calmed, and loved? Hasn't their presence added to the comfort of your home? I have often referred to this (in my own case) as feeling my husband's "John-ness". His essence, as it were. Now, the house is still, and I can feel the void he left behind.

So, on a metaphysical level, that too has been ripped from us.

Is it no wonder we feel as if we have suffered a sudden amputation and we are now dealing with a tragic bleeding stump of our life?

Now, life with our soul mate/twin flame is gone (we will discuss these terms in greater detail in just a little bit). The high of highs is gone. Our home, founded on this love of loves, has now become just a house, barren and empty. We stumble about like a war refugee among the ruins of the life we built together.

We search for the familiar, but nothing is familiar any more.

We cry out, feeling we truly can't go on.

Our lives have been turned upside down and we have no road map. We don't know what we don't know but every day we learn anew what it means to experience this awful grief.

I remember one of the times I finally understood that, when it hit home what the emptiness, the bottomless void that was made by John's death, was going to be like. It was the first summer after John had passed away, maybe just two months. I had gone out to dinner with some girlfriends in Phoenix and was driving home to Fountain Hills, a thirty-five to forty-minute drive. It was a little after nine o'clock in the evening, maybe a little later because it was already dark. And suddenly it hit me. In the past, I would have been calling John on my cell phone, letting him know that I was all right and on my way home. We would have chatted a bit, maybe we would have laughed about the latest things one of the dogs had done. He would have told me he missed me. We would have said I love you to each other and I would have felt loved, knowing he was waiting for me when I returned home.

But now, as I drove home in the dark, it came crashing down on me. No one was waiting for me at home. No one was anticipating my return with happiness. No one worried if I was late. No one would even know if I had an accident.

And then my mind wandered even further. Now there was no one in this world who knew the me that was Joy. Sure, I had friends, even some close friends. And certainly, I had family who had known me since birth. But it wasn't the same thing. There was no longer that person whose face would light up in that special way when I walked into the room. There was no one on this earth with whom I shared inside jokes, special gestures, a wonderful history, beautiful memories, and happy plans. There was no one who understood me so completely, who cheered me on when I had a new idea for a business, who believed in my abilities as John did. There was no one who made up Johnandjoy anymore and never would again. It was a horrible, sad, awful, gut-wrenching, and profoundly life-changing realization.

No wonder I felt so adrift, so bereft. The identity that I – that *we* - had built up over thirty plus years was gone – forever. Now it was just me and the losses that that implied were confounding. It was more than losing John, although that alone was horrible. I had lost our future, our everyday life, everything that made us *us*.

This is the true realization of grief and why it is so hard. And why someone becomes frustrated when they see the widow or widower fall apart months and even years after losing their spouse. They don't understand. They don't get that just because we are functioning does not mean we are healed. Yes, we are dealing with a new reality but we are forced to and we don't like it. We are still mourning what was and what can no longer be.

But despite all that, we are still here. It is not our time yet. Our story isn't finished. Our work isn't done. Despite all this sadness and loss, we must go on.

So, now what?

For starters, we have two jobs – we need to address our grief and we need to look for a way to go forward. Not move on. Remember, I hate that phrase. It's bandied about way too much, usually by those who have no understanding of what deep grief feels like. And no, that is not meant to be arrogant or condescending. It's just true. Those who are fortunate enough to have those close to them still with them on this plane just can't grasp what it means to lose their true other half. They will someday. Until then, it is our job to not only safeguard ourselves but to teach them in the process.

So, let's address that phrase "move on". Those of us who are mourning the loss of our soul mate do not want to "move on". That's the last thing we want to do. Moving on implies leaving our loved one behind, in the past and we can't and don't want to do that.

Nor should we.

No, instead we move *forward* bringing our soul mates with us into whatever new future we choose to fashion.

Joy Collins

And that is what drives my passion now. We choose to make our future – as we live with our grief. For grief is going to be part of us now. It evolves and changes as we grow. But the cure for grief is not forgetting, not getting over. The cure for grief – if there is such a thing - is to do the work of grief.

I remember when I was in the early throes of my sadness. The thing that kept coming back to me over and over was that, no matter how well I mourned, it felt as if there was no payoff. All my life I had been goal-oriented. In school, I worked hard at getting good grades and being on the honor roll. I qualified for scholarships and got into the school of my dreams. I earned my nursing degree. I interviewed to vie for jobs I wanted. I woo-ed my husband. We saved for trips and items we wanted. We applied for houses and mortgages. My point is I/we made plans and executed them for good outcomes.

But what about grief? What is the outcome for doing grief just the right way? Does grief go away? Will our soul mate walk back through that door, exclaim "That was fun!" and will life then go back to the way it was?

No, that is not going to happen. We know that.

So, what is the payoff? The answer is we must change our expectations when it comes to grief. The work of grieving is to grieve fully, to embrace our grief in all its aspects and to make it our own, not to do it according to someone else's expectations. And the desired outcome is that we learn to live with our grief, come to peace with it, make it part of our life and forge a new life *with* our grief.

I can best answer this in terms of how I dealt with it.

Grief and mourning are hard work. I had no idea just what that meant until I was faced with what it meant to have lost John. Oh, sure, we had those conversations that couples often do.

"What will you do when I die?"

"Will you remarry?"

"Will you sell the house?"

But those were fantasies for another time - a far into the future time. It was not supposed to happen when it did.

138

But it did.

And now I was looking grief square in the face and I didn't like what I saw.

Or rather what I didn't see.

I didn't see a path through this.

I didn't see how I was going to cope.

I didn't see any payoff at the end of the trail.

I didn't see an end to the trail.

What I did get was a lot of useless suggestions and equally useless platitudes.

Granted, the people offering them were truly trying to be helpful. But they didn't know they weren't being helpful. In some cases, they were making this journey harder. Harder than it needed to be.

So, I figured out soon that I was going to have to find my own way.

Along the way, I found that grief and mourning are hard work. Ultimately, it was work I had to do alone.

There were no shortcuts. In fact, research has shown that if you skip any of the work, your journey will take longer and you will eventually have to go back and do the work you skipped. That is why antidepressants don't work (unless there is a true depression overlaying the grief - but that is beyond the scope of this book. Anyone suffering from depression and/or feeling they want to harm themselves or others should seek professional help immediately. There are ways to get through that with wonderful people out there. There is no stigma in seeking this help.) But merely medicating grief to cover it up or to make it just go away only delays grief. You don't wake up one day after your pills are gone and then all is right with the world.

So, while I did seek professional help in the form of weekly and then monthly therapy with a counselor, I didn't take antidepressants.

I accepted there were things that I was just going to have to do.

139

Joy Collins

I loved.
Deeply.
Passionately.
And because I loved, now I mourned.
Deeply.
Passionately.
As you do. There is no getting around that.

I allowed myself to grieve John who was no longer physically with me in this life.

I had to come to grips with the fact I could no longer hold his hand, kiss his face, hear him snore, hug him, make love with him.......

And I cried.
Buckets.
And I ached.
As I am sure you do.
And it's hard.
But it did get better and a little easier over time.

But in that time after John passed, I allowed myself the space to mourn, knowing it was going to be hard work, keeping in mind that there was no predictable timeline.

I think that's a hard one for many. We have been told it takes a year to "get over" grief. For one thing, we have already established we don't "get over" our grief. The other thing is there is no magic number of days we should put in. Many people readily acknowledge the second year is even harder than the first year.

One of the many platitudes that was given to me after John transitioned (I like this better than died) was that time would be my new best friend.

In time, I would be "better" but it would take about a year.

In time, I would feel less sad, probably in a few months.

In time, I would "move on" and be back to my old self – again a year was mentioned.

None of that was true for me.

Grief and mourning do not fall into any set pattern or follow

140

I Will Never Leave You

any clock that I am aware of.

And while the first year is extremely difficult for many people, they hope against hope that all they must do is get through that first year and it will be easier.

Then, the second year sets in and many are surprised to find that the second year is harder than the first.

It was that way for me and I was totally unprepared. But looking back it made sense. The first year was mostly on autopilot. Just getting through the day was a chore.

The second year is when reality truly sets in and the idea that our soul mate is irretrievably forever physically gone from us in this life finally hits home.

That knowledge is heartbreaking.

And so, we begin again to mourn. Maybe not with the same soul-wrenching intensity but there are those days…

And then there are anniversaries that can trigger feelings and meltdowns – the anniversary of their passing, their birthday, your wedding day. These surges of grief can take you by surprise. After all, hasn't it been a year, eighteen months, five years? Why tears again? Why now?

Because grief has no timeline. You will mourn and heal and travel a very circuitous path from loss to making peace with your loss. It's a crooked little dance.

Never in a straight line.

Two steps forward, three steps back, one to the side and then forward again.

Honor your grief in whatever path it takes you.

Put no hard and fast expectations on yourself.

Honor your grief and the love it represents and know that you will get there in your own way, in your own time.

And it is okay.

And *that* is the payoff.

We mourn and we are made anew because we have mourned.

Because the reality is that grief has no rules.

141

Joy Collins

Years ago, Elizabeth Kubler-Ross came up with guidelines for loss: denial, anger, bargaining, depression, and acceptance, in that order.

What many people fail to remember is that this was a study initially done with those who were dying, not the experience of those who had to endure the loss of the person who died. And, to make matters more complicated, EKR herself later regretted even making this list of expectations, admitting that loss and grief indeed does NOT follow a linear and predictable progression.

Yet, to this day, her initial work is mistakenly held up to be the gold standard for grief and anyone who does not follow it is impaired in some way.

In fact, a few years ago, the psychiatric community coined the phrase "complicated grief" for anyone grieving longer than six months and suggested that these people needed psychiatric intervention.

Really? How quaint and tidy. Obviously, not the statement from anyone who has been there.

Anyone who is in the throes of mourning, especially mourning the loss of a soul mate, can readily tell you that they experience all those emotions on any given day in no particular order – heck, in any given hour, sometimes.

And to say that all is said and done in six months is pure folly.

My John has been gone a little over six years as I write this and while I admit I am in better shape today than I was way back then, there are still days that the hurt returns in full blast and I cry, and wish it weren't so, and I become upset that this has happened to us.

Is there something wrong with me? I don't think so. Not at all.

I am functioning as well as I ever did.

I take care of our home, our pets, my finances, my health.

I run a business; I keep up with family and friends; I am writing this book and have the beginnings of another on my

142

computer.

I dare anyone to say that my grief is "complicated" to the extent that I need medication and treatment.

Yet, my grief evolved in its own way and I let it and I didn't condemn myself – or allow anyone else to – when it went on for more than the amount of time others felt the need to impose on me.

When I didn't want to celebrate holidays, I didn't. When I wanted to stay home instead of going out to dinner, I did.

When I felt the need to cry and scream, I did.

And you should too.

Losing someone hurts like the dickens.

Losing your soul mate makes you feel like your heart has been ripped out of you and to some extent, it has.

Honor your feelings and don't complicate your grief by putting unrealistic – and false - expectations on it.

But once you have reached that point of allowing yourself to do the work of grief, what then?

Chapter Eighteen

☙

What then?

Then we start the next phase of our relationship with our soul mate.

And, no, I am not crazy. We do indeed still have a relationship with them. We have lost our soul mate to death. But we have not lost our soul mate. That is my message for the rest of this book.

There is not only life after death.

There is life *with our soul mate* after death.

That bears repeating –

There is life *with our soul mate* after death.

No, it's not the same. Death is real, after all. But death is a transition, not an end. Our loved ones are alive, just no longer physically with us on the three-dimensional plane of existence on the planet we call Earth. That is what I have learned and what I want to pass on to you.

Even as I was in those first few moments of John's passing I knew he continued to exist. I also knew in my heart that if any couple could continue to be together despite death, we could.

Maybe you feel that way, too.

Perhaps that is why you are reading this book.

So, let's explore this together.

As I mentioned before, within weeks after John passed, I started reading everything I could get my hands on about grief. First, I read the standard grief books. They helped – a little. But I felt there was something more I needed. I was overwhelmed with the need to know how John was, where he was, what he was doing, and how we could remain connected. It was the books on the afterlife and spirituality that finally started to give me some measure of peace and the answers I was seeking. Initially, I found myself mostly drawn to books written by mediums. I devoured books by James Van Praagh, John Holland, and George Anderson. Hearing stories about people who had had readings and contacts from the other side not only gave me comfort, it reinforced my belief that there was more to this life than what we can perceive with our five senses and that our loved ones are still with us. But I didn't limit myself to just books authored by mediums. I soon found books written by those who also did past life regressions. Then I found others who went even further and delved into that life of the soul that existed between lives. They talked about spirit guides and soul contracts. I discovered Dr. Brian Weiss, Robert Schwartz and Michael Newton.

And without even realizing it, I was not only starting to come to grips (and finally a bit of peace) with John's passing but I was starting to develop a belief system about the afterlife and our purpose for being on this earth. I was evolving as a soul and starting to do the work I needed to do to complete my soul plan.

It is my hope that by sharing what I learned with you, I can not only give you, too, some peace but help you along the way as well.

There are no coincidences.

So, let me start by summarizing what I have gleaned from

my research concerning the afterlife and this human life journey we are all on. Then I want to conclude by offering you some ideas on how you can create your own relationship with your soul mate who has died.

This summary is by no means complete and I don't claim to be an expert. I am just going to share with you what I have learned through my own studies and what I have come to believe. All I ask is that you have an open mind. Then take what you will, what resonates with you, and discard what doesn't.

Let's start with some terms.

And let's start with soul mates and twin flames. I want to spend some time on this because it's key to my belief system.

Soul mates is a term that is thrown around a lot, most often in a romantic sense. People deeply in love often tell anyone who will listen that they have found their soul mate, that they are in love for life, that nothing and no one will ever come between them and "this is *The One*". I'm sure you have heard this. You most likely, since you are reading this book, have felt that way about your mate. And it is most likely true. But did you know that technically your soul mate might not be your romantic mate/partner at all?

Let's backtrack a little.

We all have soul families – those beings with whom we travel through time, lifetime after lifetime. And yes, I firmly believe in reincarnation. It makes no sense to me that we only get one shot to get this right and then that's it – fire or bliss (I'll get into the afterlife in a bit – hang in with me). And I have experienced past life regression firsthand. It was wonderful and I will be sharing that experience as well as we go through this exploration together.

But getting back to soul families - have you ever met someone with whom you had an instant rapport? Someone who seemed familiar but you just couldn't put your finger on why? Someone who just "clicked" with you? I'm not speaking romantically. This could be a sibling, a co-worker, a fellow committee person, a friend. You get the idea. This man or woman just seemed to be on the same wavelength as you.

147

Joy Collins

Or, conversely, this person even challenged you but it was comfortable somehow.

Or perhaps there was an instant dislike and you had no rational reason for feeling that way. It was just an automatic gut feeling. This was most likely someone from your tribe, as it were. You have done this before with each other. You and this person (and there will be many who fit this description) have gone round and round, lifetime after lifetime, fulfilling roles in each other's lives. It might be for a day, an incident, a month, or a lifetime. And it could be a positive or negative role that they played in your life.

But I have also had experiences with people along the way who have hurt me and challenged me. They too have helped me, though. I believe that part of my soul plan for this lifetime has been to learn forgiveness and acceptance and these people have given me excellent ways to learn these lessons.

These people – positive and negative – are from our soul family. The roles played by our soul siblings were decided on for a reason (a soul life plan – another thing we will get into very soon).

Then, we go in further in our soul circle and we come to soul mates. What may surprise you (I know it did for me) is that you are very close to this person but not always romantically. It can be romantic. It often is. But a soul mate can also be that mentor who is always challenging you to be better, to strive higher. Or that friend who is always there for you – in the middle of the night with wine. Or that friend who just "gets" you and the two of you go on to do great things together.

I am in business right now with two women who are definitely my soul sisters/mates. Our comfort level is intense and we are all three working in the same direction with our business in a way I have never felt before. We accept each other as I have never experienced before. And we are there for each other, no matter what. Our life experiences prior to this time together have been similar in many respects, too. And now as we go forward with our business, the process is smooth and almost effortless.

You can have many soul mates and even though their job in

148

one lifetime or another may not always appear to be pleasant, the overall goal is for your highest good.

When you marry your soul mate, the relationship is intense with lots of push and pull and it may or may not last. Both partners grow from the relationship and the marriage serves a higher purpose regardless of its length.

When I married for the first time, even though that marriage had its challenges, I thought I was married to my soul mate. I probably was but that marriage didn't last more than a few years. Yet in that time, I learned a lot about myself. I became stronger, more independent, more self-assured. I was finally able to overcome my feelings of poor self-esteem that I had gathered from years of abuse in my childhood. And if that marriage hadn't happened, I would never have met John, my second husband, who was not only my soul mate but was, in fact, my Twin Flame.

I had no idea at the time when I met John that there was even such a thing as a Twin Flame. Nothing prepared me for the intensity of what we both felt. But now I know firsthand what that is. The theory behind twin flames is that at the moment of their creation they were one soul. Then they separated, as if twins formed from the same initial fertilized cell. They are true mirrors of each other, yet separate entities. Over their many lifetimes these souls grow, sometimes in the same lifetime together, sometimes not. But they always strive to ascend higher and higher spiritually. They have learned to balance their masculine and feminine aspects. Twin flames do not incarnate together very often. Their goal is to finally incarnate together when they have completed their respective spiritual learning journeys and they are ready to ascend to the next level together, possibly never needing to incarnate again on this earth plane. Thus, it is rare for a marriage to be that of a Twin Flame union. Most marriages are not. But when they are, it is truly magical.

What are some of the signs that you have met your Twin Flame? The most common sign is the feeling of instant recognition. To this day, I still remember seeing John for the first time. It was as if everyone else in the room faded into the background. My soul

149

immediately had the feeling of "There you are! Where have you been?" Yet, I fought it. So many times, I avoided being even in John's presence because the feelings were so intense and I had no idea what to do about it. His eyes seemed to see right into me. In fact, his eyes were the first thing I noticed. John, too, later told me he noticed me right away and even asked his friend who I was right after seeing me for the first time.

When we finally became a couple, it was intense from the very beginning. It was as if we had both finally come home. Instant rapport, the feeling of having known each other all our lives – and beyond. So, that is another sign – you feel an instant connection to this person. You feel comfortable sharing all aspects of your life. You may talk for hours, eager to learn everything about the other. You may find similarities in your life experiences and the things you are drawn to. You are attracted to this person in a way you have never experienced before. Your thoughts are in synch. There may be occasional separations in the relationship but ultimately, you wind up together. Your life paths merge. You work together in ways you never experienced before. This love – an intense physical and spiritual love - that develops frees each of you. There are no limitations or conditions placed on each other.

John and I were together for half my life, almost all my adult life and I am who I am today because of him. I couldn't imagine a time without him and I didn't want to experience a time without him. Yet, even in his passing, he is helping me grow and complete my soul's path. If not for his death at the very time that it happened, I would not be who I am today.

He is my Other Half. My Twin Flame.

Together we were/are one whole, yet we are separate.

Together, even when we are apart.

When you are with your Twin Flame you finally feel complete.

At peace. Home.

And speaking of Home brings me to the Afterlife, our true Home. Let's talk about that next.

Chapter Nineteen
CB

Most of us have grown up with an interpretation of the Afterlife that was given to us and we just took for granted as correct. Whether from our parents, or school, or Church, or a combination of all of that – it was something that we most likely accepted as true because it was all we knew. And there is nothing wrong with that. It's a good way to start. But there comes a time when you must look back on that and see if it still works for you.

I was raised Roman Catholic from birth – baptized at an age when I was too young to know what that meant, then on to Catholic grammar school and Catholic high school. I don't regret any of that. It was an excellent education. But then, after that, came a time when I rejected all that and didn't follow any religion even though I still believed what I had been taught – which was sad because it was all about guilt and rejection and sin and lack of love.

Then, in the summer of 1985, I had a health crisis and came back to the Church. John joined me in our faith, he converted to Catholicism, and we remarried in the Church. We worshipped

Joy Collins

together and that helped us grow together. After that, we were lucky to be introduced to some new spiritual concepts through good friends. The lessons of *The Secret* and *The Celestine Prophecy* helped us tremendously. That was followed by finding *The Conversations with God* series of Neale Donald Walsch and the writings of Paramahansa Yogananda.

And one thing led to another, each building on the other. We both remained Catholic – and I still am – but we added a more spiritual component to our faith based on love, not fear. The post-graduate course for me though occurred after John passed when I started reading everything I could get my hands on about the Afterlife and what we are meant to learn from our time here on Earth.

So, now I want to distill all of that for you into a coherent format, explaining what I have come to believe so we can build on it as we go forward in this book together.

First off, I no longer believe in Hell, per se. Even the current Pope has acknowledged this. Hell and its fire was made up to help early believers follow the straight and narrow through fear. But think about that for a moment. If God loves us unconditionally, why would He make a place like Hell? Sure, we can say we choose to be in Hell by our actions but is that the case? Remember how Catholics were not supposed to eat meat on Friday and if they knowingly did, they would go to Hell for all eternity unless they confessed to it?

Really? Do you think God cares about that? Do you think eating meat on Friday is just as bad as killing your fellow man? That being said, I do believe in lower realms and we do send ourselves there by our actions in this life. The difference (I believe) is that we have the chance to work our way out of these lower realms once we become aware, either by actions we perform in the flesh or work we do in spirit.

Heaven is not a place we are meant to get to through fear. God is Love with a capital L. We are created out of His love. Our journey is supposed to help us get back to God/Love. No matter how long it takes. Remember we have eternity to get this right.

Our lives and our interactions with each other are based on

love – or our lack of it. The punishment we receive – if we can call it that – is based on our inability to love. We experience what we made in this life – and all our other lives.

So, maybe I need to back track even more.

Yes, as I said before, I believe in reincarnation. It just makes no sense to me that we get only one turn at bat and, win or lose, our fate is determined for all eternity. And today there are plenty of stories and books out there depicting evidence of this.

Reincarnation was a universal belief up until the time it was banned by the early Christian church. Again, this was to instill fear and compliance. The thought was if people believed they had many lives, maybe they wouldn't do things right this time around (whatever time they were in) because they knew they could try again.

But again, if God is infinite Love, why would He do that to us, the children He loves, the souls He created to be with Him? He is not the vengeful bearded person on high passing out judgment as He has so often been depicted. In fact, He is not passing out judgment at all. We are.

Say what?

We create our reality in the Afterlife through karma.

So, what exactly is karma?

Have you ever heard someone smugly claim to forgive someone who had wronged them because they knew karma was going to "get" that person in the end? They were partially right. Although the thing about karma is it is not about the other person.

Karma is about us.

The idea of karma is a Buddhist concept but it has become mainstream even though it is still fairly misunderstood in the Western world, in my opinion. Karma is not the idea of bad actions forming negative energy and coming back to bite our foes in the spiritual butt. It is not something we sit back and gleefully wait for our enemies to endure. Karma is all about us.

Our karma.

And that is all that matters.

Let me give you an example.

153

A few years ago, I hired a gentleman to do some work on my house. I paid him up front for supplies and for most of the labor. Yes, it was a stupid move on my part. But he was a son of a friend who had been there for me after John had passed and I felt I owed her for that. I appreciated what she had done for me and I wanted to do something nice for her in return. Her son had had some difficulties in his life. So, out of compassion for my friend and, looking back, a displaced sense of obligation, I wanted to help him get back on his feet. Within weeks of receiving my money, he was gone. Apartment abandoned, checks cashed. Nowhere-to-be-found-gone.

And I was out thousands of dollars. Upsetting? You bet, to say the least. Sputtering anger, imagining all the things I could do to him if I ever saw him again, was more like it.

The next instinct of course would be for me to gloat and say karma was going to get him. And, truth be told, he possibly had built up some negative karma by choosing to behave that way. But there are several things at work here. First, he and I might have agreed to this chain of events when we made a map of this lifetime. So, if that is so, then it forces me to look at the bigger picture. What is the lesson here for me? Not for him but for me? My karma is determined by my reaction. If I harbor anger and hold onto that, I am building up resentment and negative karma and I am not learning the lesson of forgiveness.

And keep in mind that forgiveness doesn't imply that what he did was all right. It's not. But that is not the focus here. The focus is my soul and my soul's growth. If I work on forgiveness, I am growing. I am elevating my karma. I am working through the life task of forgiving so that I don't have to go through that trial again and can move on to other issues. My task is to forgive him, wish him well, and let it go. Dwelling on what he did will only hurt me.

In examining my own life, I find a pattern where certain situations have shown up and I have been given the opportunity to become bitter and resentful and angry or to look beyond the event in front of me and learn to forgive. I'm not saying it was easy. I was angry for various reasons for a very long time. But there is a saying attributed to Buddha: "Holding onto anger is like drinking poison and expecting the other person to die." I think this is very true. Who is being hurt by my anger? In most cases, it's not the other guy. There are certain aspects of my childhood that could make me very bitter if I want to dwell on them. Certainly, the physical and emotional abuse of my first marriage qualifies for an angry reaction. And there are other instances. I'm sure you can find several in your own life as well.

But answer this: who does it harm if you stay angry?

When those nine individuals were killed in the church in South Carolina in 2015, family members of the deceased surprised many people by standing up in court and verbalizing forgiveness to the killer. They were not being weird or strange. They were practicing compassion and love. It wasn't about the killer. It was about them and their souls. And they were also instrumental in modeling forgiveness for others. Who knows the number of people they may have touched that day by their actions? They may have done more good by their example than they will ever know. How the murderer goes about the rest of his life will determine his karma. It is none of anyone's business but his.

But our own karma has far-reaching effects for us.

At the very least it determines the level of the growth of our soul. And that brings me back to our discussion of the Afterlife.

Our soul's level of growth determines where we live in the Afterlife – at least in the immediate time after we die. Our experience of the Afterlife (told to us by those who have experienced it either through near-death experience or more in depth by those who have channeled information to us through highly evolved souls such as mediums) is determined by two things. In the immediate time after death, what we perceive Heaven to be is determined by our preference here on Earth. For instance, if we think it is churches and choirs singing, we will most likely experience that until we know enough not to.

But secondly, and more importantly, our Afterlife experience, or Heaven if you prefer, is determined by the degree to which the lessons we set out to learn in this lifetime have been

Joy Collins

learned. Our soul's positive energy level at the moment of our death is the level at which we start our Heavenly journey on the Other Side.

So, let's go on to explore what those who have tapped into the Other Side have told us.

Quantum physics teaches us that all life, indeed all matter, is energy and vibration. The more we drill down to the basic components of what we observe, the more fantastic it appears.

Take the chair you are sitting on right now, for example. It appears to you to be solid and unmoving. Yet, if you observed the wood, for instance, it would be composed of atoms that are largely made up of space. Electrons and neutrons, et cetera, but lots of space in between. It is the degree of vibration that determines how solid something appears to be.

We here on Earth are vibrating at a lower frequency giving us the illusion of things being solid and unmoving. But as scientists have learned, all matter is composed of atoms and energy or vibration. The more spiritual and loving we strive to become on this earthly plane, the higher our vibration. And the higher our vibration, the higher the level we start out at in the next life.

It sounds simple but it is far from easy. Earth is a tough school. That's why we chose it.

And yes, we chose this life. That may be hard to understand or accept but that is exactly what happened when we set out on this trip around.

So, before I go on any more about the nature of the Afterlife, let's stop a minute and talk about our soul plan, the story we chose to work on in this life. This might be a new concept to you – or might not. But for the sake of discussion, let's assume we are learning about this together.

"Things are happening the way they are supposed to." That was John's favorite saying. I agreed with him in theory, but I always thought it meant that the Universe was allowing things to happen so that we could learn and grow. That it was something "out there". I believed that what John meant was that what was happening was the Universe or God's plan, that I was an innocent victim or bystander, as the case may be. Many people subscribe to this, claiming that "God doesn't give us more than we can handle". Well, that sounds cruel, sometimes, because some people seem to be God's least favorite people or his little scapegoats. And I don't believe that of God for a minute.

No, now, after losing John and embarking on this phase of my journey, I have a different perspective.

I have read a wonderful book called *Your Soul's Plan* by Robert Schwartz. I highly recommend it. It talks about pre-birth planning and how we, as eternal loving souls, plan what we are going to experience in this life. Then, with our Guides and with other souls from our "family/group", we all agree to participate and play certain roles to help each other with our individual life lessons.

I also believe there is a second part to this planning. I believe that most of the souls who have incarnated right now are here for a higher purpose as well. As I am sure you have noticed, our planet is in turmoil. But it is also in the process of a great awakening. You are probably part of that awakening. The fact that you are open to expanding your knowledge of the Other Side and communicating with those who have passed attests to that. Those who are interested in these metaphysical topics are the ones who will lead the way for others, expanding love on this planet and ushering in the next phase – a heaven on earth.

But that is a bigger story for another day. Just put that thought in your mind and let it germinate. I guarantee you if you let it, it will guide you to more knowledge on that subject. It will come to you in its own time, when it's supposed to.

But for now, let's address our relationship with our soul mates.

When I look at life from the perspective of soul planning, John's favorite saying takes on new meaning for me.

"Things are happening the way they are supposed to."

Was John telling me that he and I had agreed to this? That his death was supposed to happen when it did and I was supposed to go on and do work because of that occurring? Was I now to understand that he had finished his plan but I am still here to complete mine? If that is the case, it gives me a measure of peace. Nothing bad is happening. Things are just happening as we agreed to and when he and I are together again, all will be well.

And I truly believe that if I just reach out with my heart and soul with love, we can still reach each other. He is only a thought away. We are still together and we are doing this together. Just as we planned.

As I have mentioned several times, reincarnation just makes sense to me. Each time we come through, our goal is to work on issues that help us get closer and closer to God or Source on the Other Side. We do this by choosing lessons that are important to us and to the growth of our soul. These topics, if you will, are carefully decided upon with the help of our Guides before we incarnate.

But I do not claim to be an expert on this. Not by any means. I have come to this conclusion because of my own research and through past life regression experiences. I have also read that these lives we experience are not linear (one happening after another in sequence) but rather all at once. Since Time does not exist on the Other Side, perhaps this is true. I can't say. The more I delve into this, the more questions I have.

But maybe I am wrong to say Time does not exist on the Other Side. Maybe it's just not as we know it. Wasn't it Albert Einstein who said "Time is relative"? And it is indeed. I look back on my early years with John. From the moment I first met him until the day we married was just a little less than five years. It seemed as if we crammed so much into that short space of time - meeting, becoming friends, falling in love, moving in together, marrying.

Yet, now, it has been just a little over six years since John has passed and there are days I feel it is all the same and at the end of the day, the only constant is John is still gone. The days and nights are still empty. There are no hugs and kisses, no plans, no milestones.

Those first five years flew by.

These last six years have crawled past.

One of my favorite recent movies is "Interstellar". During their trip into space, the astronauts spend time on a planet researching its habitability. Because of gravity issues too complicated to go into here, every hour spent on the surface of the planet equals seven years to the astronaut left back on the ship orbiting the planet. The astronauts on the planet's surface run into trouble and their return is delayed by over three hours. When they return to their ship, twenty-three years have passed and their colleague has visibly aged.

Sometimes I feel that way. As of this writing John has been gone for a little more than six years and there are days it feels like forever. I wonder how it feels for him. Has it been only an hour in Heavenly terms? When we are reunited will it seem to him like he just left?

Something to think about.

But let's continue. My purpose in discussing any of the Afterlife is only to get to my real purpose in writing this book which is to discuss how we can bridge the divide between us and our soul mates and other loved ones who have passed over.

But while we are discussing reincarnation let me throw out some things for you to consider.

As I just mentioned, our world is in great turmoil right now. Instead of coming together, we seem to be drifting further and further apart. Our differences – or at least what we perceive to be our differences - seem to be dividing us. But what we perceive as our differences only exist as products of our senses. Underneath we are all souls, genderless and colorless souls. And souls without adherence to one set religion. All of those are man-made differences. One of the interesting things I experienced during past-life regression is that I have been male in some lifetimes. I have also been a female priest, a shaman if you will. And who knows what other lives I have lived? If that is the case, does it really matter what human form I am in now? What religion I follow? What sex I exhibit in this body? Who I choose to love in this body? When looked at from that perspective, our differences vanish. And hating each other because of those differences becomes meaningless. And yes, stupid.

I also remember having a brief flash of insight once while just lying in bed with John. I don't remember the circumstances but

159

Joy Collins

we were lying there quietly next to each other and I had a sudden realization that he and I were two souls that were forever connected but were neither male or female to each other. We just were. That was many years ago, but I can still remember that instant very clearly. It made that much of an impression on me.

Ram Dass, the author of *Be Here Now*, once said "We're all just walking each other home." And that's true. I used to watch a very interesting TV series called "Drop Dead Diva". The premise of the series is that a woman dies, goes to heaven, and wants to come back so she hits the return button on her guardian angel's computer. The problem is she comes back into a recently vacated body, not her own, and must live a different life. It's a little more complicated than that but I think you get the idea. The episodes revolved around her complications from this premise as well as legal/crime cases since she came back as an attorney (she had been a model before).

The interesting part happened in the last season when the same thing happened to her boyfriend. He died and then came back as well because he couldn't stand to be away from her. And yes, he came back as someone else. They found each other and learned to love each other again in new bodies and new circumstances. The whole series was a kind of a microcosm of reincarnation and soul mates.

I know - this sounds crazy. But trust me, it was handled well and made for an interesting series. But it brings up the bigger issue that I am trying to explain in an imperfect way.

Here's another example from television. I'm a big Star Trek fan. And one of my favorite versions of that whole genre was the series *Star Trek – The Next Generation*. I loved their stories that examined the human condition and all its permutations. And one of my favorite stories involved the ship's doctor, Beverly Crusher. The episode was called "The Host." In it, Dr. Crusher falls in love with an alien named Odan who has come on board to mediate a dispute between two warring planets. He appears to be a humanoid of sorts and the romance becomes quite steamy over the course of a couple of weeks. Then Odan is fatally injured and during his treatment, Odan confesses to Beverly that he is a joined species, that the body

160

she knows as Odan is just a host (from the Trill planet) and the real Odan is a slug-like being living inside of him that must now be transferred to a new host body before the host dies. A new host body is many hours away and to keep the Odan-being alive, it is temporarily transferred into the body of William Riker, the number two in command and a friend of Dr. Crusher. After some misgivings, Beverly then continues her romance with Odan/Riker. After successfully completing the mediation, Odan is removed from Riker. By this time, the new host body arrives. Except now, the host is a female from the Trill planet. Once the transfer is completed, the new Odan/Trill wishes to continue the relationship with Dr. Crusher but she is unable to get past this new development and they part ways.

Of course, this was just a story. But it was a beautiful allegory for reincarnation. Our souls are like the Odan slug, going from body to body. The outer shell changes but underneath we are still us. We are truly just souls underneath. That is the real us.

Bodies don't matter.

Gender doesn't matter.

Sexual preference doesn't matter.

Religious choice doesn't matter.

And our "stories" don't matter either.

Our spirits/souls *do* matter and what we do with our lives in terms of the love we give.

Bottom line is - Love is all there is.

That is what we hear repeatedly from those who have crossed over to the Other Side.

Carrying this further - weight doesn't matter. Money doesn't matter. Toys don't matter. Cars, homes, stocks, prestige, position - none of it matters. What matters is that we love.

I know I have developed a different perspective on life since John has passed. Losing him has made me realize how fleeting all this is. If there has been a gift in his passing it is this. And I am grateful for the gift.

So, back to our discussion. If we accept the premise of reincarnation and plans for each incarnation, we then must address

161

how we plan these excursions to Earth with our spiritual team and guides. Who are our Guides? We usually have a whole team of guides. They can be loved ones who have passed on, angels who are assigned to us for this lifetime, and highly evolved souls or Masters who have helped us in this life and most likely, previous lives as well.

I will give you an example from my own experience.

I underwent my series of past life regressions with medium Susanne Wilson. Susanne is known as the Carefree Medium (she lives in Carefree Arizona) and while she has had her gift since she was a child she has only been actively practicing as a medium for the past several years, since she had her own near-death experience.

Susanne is a wonderful mentor and I have learned so much from her. My experiences with intuition development and past life regression have changed my life. Undergoing past life regression was not only fascinating but very informative. I could experience myself as my Soul Being, not just as Joy. Joy is who I am this time around. But my true Soul is a wiser being, a more grounded being. I was able to see the lives I have experienced from a more detached point of view. I saw them as stories with purpose without all the anxiety and emotion most of us go through on a day to day basis.

I have gone through three past life regression sessions so far. In the first two, I experienced six different earlier lifetimes. No, I wasn't the Queen of Egypt or a famous Revolutionary War hero. That kind of thing only happens in books and movies. Most of us have had very ordinary lives. The trick is to learn the lessons from each one and to ascertain if we accomplished what we set out to do.

I must admit I was not always very successful in the lives I observed. In fact, in a few of those lives, I failed miserably. Which brings me to my last past life session. In that one, I explored the time between lives, specifically the time before this incarnation whereby I made the plans for what I was going to experience and why. And during that session I came to know my own team. One of them is Charles, my Master Guide, a highly evolved soul who has been with me as my Guide through several lifetimes, perhaps all of them. The rest of my team (that I have learned about so far – there may be more) is comprised of my two guardian angels Stephen and Enoria, Archangel Michael, and John. Also, at that planning meeting was Bill, my ex-husband who has also passed. Bill obviously belongs to my soul family and he was there to plan his part in my life this time around. During this session, I learned what I intended on accomplishing in this life and what roles people were going to play. I agreed to certain events. No, things were not prearranged down to every detail. I still have free will. Only the major events were discussed. I reviewed what my goals were going to be and what I wanted to learn.

But when we incarnate, we forget all this. While the events play out, it is up to us at the time they occur to react in the moment. That is where we build up positive or negative energy, our karma. Yes, it seems counter-intuitive that we don't remember the plan but how else will we learn? If we know the events to come and what our reaction should be, there is no learning. Our souls can't grow. And that is the whole point of being here. The good thing is though, if we pay attention, if we educate ourselves and then start to look for lessons, then things become clearer, more and more.

That is why we see an increase in awakening on this planet now. More and more people are becoming aware. And the more we become aware, the more we become aware. And once we become aware, we can never not be aware ever again.

Cool, huh?

So, to get back to my plan – I observed the discussions I had with John about what he and I were going to do this time around. I have always known/felt that John was my true soul mate/twin flame and that has been confirmed to me repeatedly in both my past life regressions and in this observed pre-life planning session.

Has that made what I have experienced easier? Yes, to some extent. However, I am still sad to be widowed from John. I miss him terribly. But I also know I have work to do. And I know why I have that work to do. This book is part of that work. I also know that I am not alone. I have my team with me and I can call on any of them at any time. This earth life is school. And when I am done, I will go Home.

Chapter Twenty

ℭℬ

So - back to our discussion of Home, the Afterlife.

Unless someone has died, no one knows for sure what that is like. But we do have the stories of those who have died and come back, those people who have had near death experiences. And we have had messages given to us by our loved ones through mediums. And there have been books written by people who have "channeled" from those who have passed on. Based on all of that we can make a compilation of what we believe the afterlife to be.

So, let me see if I can summarize our discussion.

The Afterlife is made up of several levels. And our place in it is based on how well we did in this life, as we already discussed. In the past, people have always pointed upward when referring the "where" of Heaven. Is that where it is? Who knows? Some people have said we are all occupying the same place at the same time just in different dimensions. I don't claim to know that answer. I'm willing to find that out when the time comes.

Joy Collins

The other confusing thing (for those of us in body) is that there is no such thing as time on the Other Side. For me, who has always been acutely aware of time, this seems an impossibility. But again, I am willing to go along with that. Frankly, it seems like a nice thing.

So, to sum up so far, in the Afterlife there is a lack of time and a different concept of space and place. So far, pretty confusing, right?

But that is probably a reflection of our earthly frame of reference that we need to define Heaven in terms of time and physical attributes. Those who have had near-death experiences (NDE's) and those who have been in contact with those who have passed tend to concentrate not so much on "the what" as they do on the feelings.

They describe unconditional Love and non-judgment. They talk about being back with all their loved ones who have passed. They talk about a life review where they see not only the good they did but also the harm they caused and the missed opportunities. And they experience it from the perspective of those they affected by their behavior - something to seriously consider the next time we harm someone.

Anita Moorjani in her book *Dying to be Me* describes the NDE she experienced when she fell into a coma. She claims Heaven is a state of being, not a place. And she also describes in great detail the feeling of love and oneness with everyone and everything around her.

My personal belief is that Heaven is both a place *and* a feeling, if that is what we choose. John has shown me in dreams the house where he lives now and what he has prepared for us for when I return (more on this in the next chapter).

I have also come to learn through my soul planning session that I have a job on the other side and part of what I chose to experience during this time around on Earth was chosen on purpose so that I can do a better job after I pass. Looking back on what I have experienced so far, I could choose to be very upset and depressed.

166

Things have not always gone well and I have endured some very sad and hurtful episodes. But now, if I look at them as things I chose with a purpose in mind, it doesn't seem so bad.

And no, I am not putting a Pollyanna-like face on it and saying everything is peaches and cream and I don't hurt. I do hurt. Some days, I hurt a lot. But I am determined to make my life useful and do and be the best I can be so that when I do transition I can look back and know I did what I came to do and I can walk into that house with John and start on the next phase of our journey together, doing good on the Other Side and working ever closer on my relationship with God/Source.

It all sounds exciting to me.

But for now, you and I are still here and while all the talk of the Afterlife sounds very optimistic, we are still left with our grief, aren't we?

We still miss our soul mates and that hurts.

Remember I said a while back that we are still in relationship with our soul mates? I wasn't kidding.

So, now, with all this past discussion as framework, let's talk about what I want to spend the rest of this book on – how we can stay in relationship with our soul mates while we are still in this life.

What I am about to discuss will hopefully help you in your grieving process as well. No, it's not going to take it away. Grief is something we must endure. It's not something we can skip over or rush or medicate away.

But the severity of our grief can be mitigated. In fact, if we can decrease the intensity of it at some point it will allow us to be more receptive to receiving communication from our loved ones. The energy of intense grief can sometimes block that communication.

I belong to several afterlife groups on Facebook and many times those who are in grief will write in and say they need a sign from their loved one. They go on to explain that they are not able to sleep, they are crying every day, and they are convinced something is wrong because they are not getting a sign. If only they would get

167

a sign. Why aren't their loved ones communicating? Is something wrong?

The desperation leaps off the page and I totally sympathize. I remember my own feelings those first horrible days after John passed. I screamed to the heavens "Where are you?" and "How are you?" in between begging John to just come back.

Little did I know John was already reaching out to me.

So, let's go through the various ways we can get communication from our loved ones. And keep in mind I am not saying we can have physical conversations with our soul mates – although I have heard of people who do. I myself have gotten the occasional sentence but this is not common. What I am going to explain are just ways that our other halves will be able to reach out and do something as simple as say in their own way "I'm still here. I love you."

And if we can recognize these various "Hello's", as I like to call them, we can be reassured our soul mates/twin flames/loved ones are not only still alive but still with us. We can continue to be in relationship with them.

It's not perfect but it will help assuage our grief and make life more bearable until we are reunited with them.

The major ways I have found this communication to continue is with dreams, various presents (like feathers and coins), energy manifestations (such as orbs, interfering with electrical equipment), and other miscellaneous messages (such as songs, license plates, times on a clock). Finally, I will briefly discuss meditating, and just plain listening. I can only touch on these topics enough to show you that they work. If you want to go into depth with any of them, I will have some information for you on how to go about doing that too.

So, let's begin.

Chapter Twenty-One

CB

Let's start with dreams.

This is probably one of the more well-known ways for spirit communication. Time and time again, I have heard from those who are mourning say they have dreamt of their loved ones and the dream seemed "so real". That's because in all likelihood, it was not a dream but a true visit.

My metaphysical teachers have told me that when we sleep, we are more receptive to the energy of the afterlife and can have wonderful adventures. Those more highly evolved souls report traveling to other dimensions and attending school where they learn what they need to advance their soul.

But for our purposes we are going to explore how you can visit with your loved one while you are in the dream state.

As I mentioned earlier in my story, I had what I thought was a very vivid dream the first night after John had passed. John came to me and we finally had the good-bye we weren't able to have earlier that day. It's personal and I won't go into the details but it felt very real. The dream had none of the qualities that some dreams do where things don't make sense and people and objects appear strange. John had substance, for lack of a better word. The impressions were so vivid I remember them to this day. But when I awoke, while I was happy to have been in John's presence I thought it was just a very realistic and vivid dream. I didn't know then as I do know now about dream visits and instead chalked it up to my driving need to have John back with me.

Since that first night, I have had several of these visits from John on the Other Side.

I have already told you what is probably my favorite one involving his backpack as well as a few others over the course of this book. One of them even involved our cat Charlotte.

Here is just one more and then I want to explain why these are visits and not "just dreams". This last dream I want to tell you about is one where I think John was allowing me to experience where he is right now and where we will be once I transition. The dream occurred over a year ago, but I can see it in my mind even now.

I remember the last scene especially. I was on a street that felt familiar and I was walking home when I came to what I "felt" was my/our house. At first, I thought there was snow on the trees and then I looked closer and I could see that everything was coming into bloom. And what I had thought was snow on the ground was actually flower petals strewn all over. There were pink flowers everywhere I looked. There was a dogwood tree out front and rhododendron bushes - all turning pink with flowers. I remember feeling so happy. It was breathtakingly beautiful. The front door of the house was open and I could see into the kitchen beyond but I couldn't see John and I remember wondering where he was.

Then I looked toward the backyard and I could see the top of his head just over a block wall. He looked up when he heard me approach and he smiled that smile I know so well. I waved. I was so happy to see him. He laughed as if he had something good to tell me and he motioned for me to come into the house and then he started to go in. I moved toward the front door and that's when I woke up. I woke up feeling so happy and content. This is where I believe we will be living when we are back together.

So, what do all these dreams have in common?

I am not alone in feeling I have visited with a loved one in a dream after their death. This is a phenomenon that has been around for probably centuries and studied extensively. Books have been written about it. And anyone who talks about communication from those who have passed eventually gets around to talking about dream visits.

Why are they so common?

What separates a dream visit from just an everyday run-of-the-mill dream?

There seem to be certain characteristics common to these types of dreams.

But first let's talk a little bit about how and why they happen. Or at least what the consensus is. No one obviously can say for sure but based on some pretty good research and hundreds, if not thousands of reports, we can come to some consistent conclusions.

As we have already discussed our loved ones who have passed "live" on another plane or dimension. Most often this is referred to as the astral plane and it is made of energy. When we sleep, we are open to that dimension. We are more receptive. Our loved ones can reach us on that energy/thought plane.

And why is obvious. In this life, when we are away from loved ones, isn't it almost instinctive to want to communicate with those we have left behind to tell them we have arrived at our destination, we are well, and we love those we miss?

It is the same for our loved ones who have passed; certainly, for our soul mates who know only too well how much we are mourning their passing.

So, they enter our minds during our dream state and we can "visit".

How do you know if these dreams are in fact visits?

171

Consistently these dreams have characteristics unlike what we call ordinary dreams. Everyone has had those crazy wild dreams that you think about as soon as you wake up and ask "What was THAT all about?" - those are the dreams that make no sense and drift away as soon as your head clears and you start the day.

But dreams that are visits from our loved ones and soul mates who have passed are very different. They consistently share the same descriptions:

1 – A sense of touch and/or reality – I remember the first thing that made me sit up and take notice was that I could "feel" John. If he hugged me or squeezed me in an embrace, it was real, as real as if a person were to do that in my waking state. Often, I awoke still feeling his touch on my skin. In that dream where I found his backpack left behind on the bench, I remember picking it up, feeling the leather on my fingers, and the sense of the papers rustling inside it. Other laws of reality also apply. There is no morphing of objects, no underwater swimming with mermaids, no flying over skyscrapers.

2 – Our loved ones are happy. They smile. They convey to us that they are all right. They usually look younger and healthy.

3 – These dreams stay with us. They don't fade away as our day goes on. In fact, people report still remembering these types of dreams months and years later in full detail. I know I do. I can still feel how John held me and told me he was never going to leave me again in one visit. I know exactly where his hand was on my arm. I cherish what he told me.

4 – Sometimes, these dreams will relay a message. Again, going back to my dream about his backpack, John was clearly telling me that I needed to get it from his locker at work. I had forgotten all about it and I have no idea if I ever would have remembered it if he hadn't shown that to me. This occurred three months after his death and it is now over six years and I still remember details of that visit.

5 – Communication may not be verbal but it will always be clear and understood. Sometimes, the messages conveyed will appear to be telepathic but we will easily understand our loved one.

6 – The dream visit will always leave you with a sense of peace and love. My cousin Claudia told me that she had a definite feeling of closure after John visited her in that dream about a month after he passed. He told her that it was his time to go and he didn't want her to be sad. She said she felt his hug (she always loved his hugs) and when she awoke she knew he was okay and that she was going to be okay too. While she still missed him, she knew she could now heal. Sometimes, my dream visits from John make me a little sad upon awakening but that is only because I wished I could have dreamed longer about him. I cherish every one of the times he has come to me and the feelings of love stay with me for hours, if not days. Who am I kidding? I still feel his love and I am grateful for the times we get to spend like that. It is a true gift.

Chapter Twenty-Two
CB

Next to dreams, perhaps the most often reported signs of communication that people describe are what I like to call "presents".

These are physical objects that can come in many forms and are recognized and most meaningful when they are specific between the two people – us on this side and our loved one the other side. Because of that, we can't limit that only one or two objects are definite presents and all others are just wishful thinking. There is no end to what can comprise a present.

However, I will go over the usual ones and explain about how you can tell if what you have noticed and received is a present for you specifically. And I will help illustrate by giving you some examples from my own experience.

The most reported gifts that our loved ones send us are feathers and coins. The key to recognizing these symbols as truly coming from our soul mates and not just some random occurrence is when and how it happens. For instance, if you live in a bird sanctuary then finding a feather is not a message. But let's say you are thinking about your loved one and then happen to look down as you enter your car and there on the ground is a beautiful feather, all by itself. Chances are it's a wonderful Hello.

I can think of a couple of times when this happened to me.

In the first instance, I had been ruminating about a situation with my car. I had been in an accident a couple of months prior and the frame of my car had been damaged. While it had been expertly repaired, I was worried whether I should trade it in, if for no other reason than future safety. John was very particular about the condition of our cars. He worked on them himself and was very knowledgeable about cars in general. I always turned to him for car advice and was now wishing I had him with me to ask about what I should do.

So, on the way to visit my chiropractor just one day after getting my car back from the repair shop, I was mulling over the pros and cons of trading the car in. I was afraid I was being foolish and shouldn't spend the extra money on a new car. But my gut feeling was that I should not keep the car but rather trade it in for a newer model, free of the worry of any residual damage from the accident.

Then, just as I got out of my car at the chiropractor's office, a beautiful dragonfly (often another sign) buzzed around me. In fact, he slammed right into my driver's side door after I got out of the car. I thought that was odd, but he flew away, only to return a second later and buzz me again. So, I paid attention. Then, I took a step forward and there, sticking straight up out of the front lawn ahead of me was a large black feather. Those can't have both been coincidences so close together. I knew in my heart it was John and he was trying to reassure me that I was making the right decision.

Here's one more example. Since I live alone now, I am frequently concerned about noises at night. You know, those things that go bump in the night and convince you that the end is near. On one evening, while watching television at around nine o'clock, I heard what I thought were strange thumping noises over near one corner of my house, right where the electrical box is. To make matters worse, the television then just turned off.

At first, I thought the noise was one of the cats in another room but all three of them were in the room with me and two of them picked up their heads and looked in the direction of the noise. And that didn't account for the TV going off. I live out in a rural area of Arizona and after dark there are critters about that I don't care to run into, so I was reluctant to go outside to check. I ran through the footage on the security cameras I have and didn't see anything amiss. I also looked out all the windows on that side of the house and because of our outdoor lighting I could see that there was no sign of danger. I hoped it was just an animal and convinced myself to go back to watching my show and not worry about it.

But, of course, it did weigh on my mind and the next morning I went around to that side of the house to look. I found nothing wrong and nothing that could tell me why I heard a noise or had a sudden loss of power. But there on the ground right near the electrical box was a beautiful feather, just lying there by itself. John had told me through a medium once that he watches over me in the house. I believe that feather was his way of reminding and reassuring me.

I kept the feather.

But feathers may not be what your loved one sends you. Perhaps it is coins – pennies, nickels, dimes. Often, if you check the date on the coin you may find that it is significant. Others report finding other objects that are meaningful.

John used to write little love notes to me on sticky notes. Over the years I had saved them and placed them in various drawers around the house for safekeeping, often forgetting that they were even there. In the years after John's passing, they have somehow managed to make their way back to the front of those drawers, sticking up in obvious ways when I open them. You can imagine how happy it makes me feel to see these little reminders of him.

Let me give you one last example of this phenomenon before we move on.

Sparkles have always meant something special to John and me. I think most people call them glitter; we called them sparkles. But regardless of what you call them, I don't think anyone can look at those little pieces of light and not feel good. Our special connection to glitter came about at a St. Patrick's Day party many years ago. The circumstances are personal and not important to the story except that for the rest of our life together whenever John and I saw glitter we looked at each other with that look that partners share and we would smile.

Since John's passing, he continues to share that "look" with me. I have found glitter in places that glitter would never have ordinarily found itself. I have no other explanation other than it is John's doing.

Here are some instances:

- On John's sixty-ninth birthday a piece of glitter just appeared on my keyboard. As I watched it, it faded in and out of existence and then eventually was just gone.
- On my way to pick up the memory quilt that I had had made from some of John's shirts, I found a piece of gold glitter on my driver's seat. On another occasion, there was one on my steering wheel.
- One day while vacationing in Sedona, I asked John for a sign that he was all right. I was sitting in a hotel restaurant and looked down at my table and there was a piece of glitter right in front of me and "I'll Be Home for Christmas" was playing on the loudspeaker. That song has always tugged at my heart.
- I was diagnosed with Valley Fever back in June 2014 and was understandably quite upset about it. Plus, I was feeling physically awful and wishing John were with me so I would have his support and love. He always made things more bearable plus he took such

good care of me. Anyway, I was thinking about all of that and then found a piece of glitter on my slippers. The odd thing was I had just washed them so there was no rational reason for that to have been there.

And one more story –

Last summer we had a very strong storm with lots of violent wind. It was so strong that it damaged one of the ceiling fans on our deck. That led to it shorting out when I turned it on to take my dog out for her last potty break one Friday evening, which in turn flipped the breaker causing some other lights in the house to go out as well. I was going to ignore it but John had other plans. The idea of going to bed and attending to it the next morning just didn't feel right so I called the emergency line for my electrician. They sent someone to check it out even though by now it was 10:30 at night. His name turned out to be Gabriel. Honest! While this whole incident was unfolding, I had been texting my two friends, Cathy and Betts, keeping them up to date with this latest house adventure. Cathy kept insisting this whole lights going out thing was John's doing. I said it couldn't have been. Why would John want my lights to go out?

Turns out, Cathy was right. While Gabriel investigated the source of the problem, he found a bigger issue. The electrical boxes the deck ceiling fans were mounted to were in the process of physically breaking. They were the initial ones put in when the house was built back in 1984 and were not meant for the weight of the outdoor fans. The brackets were already cracked and crumbling. If Gabriel hadn't found them when he did the fans were destined to fall and some serious injury could have occurred. Probably to me.

So, he took the fans down before they fell, capped off the wires and we made plans to replace the fans with new boxes on the following Monday.

While I was waiting for Gabriel to clean up and come back with the bill, I busied myself by cleaning the kitchen counter where I found one single sparkle shining up at me. I smiled. Once again, John was watching over me and the house. And that piece of glitter was his way of letting me know.

179

Joy Collins

So, to sum up – these little physical signs that our loved ones give us can take many forms. They can be lasting or can disappear after they've given their message (when this happens, they are called apports). The only rule is they must be meaningful to us at the moment. You will know in your heart when it is a true sign and not just an ordinary occurrence. Not every feather or coin – or piece of glitter – is a present. But the ones that are will be cherished.

Chapter Twenty-Three

CB

Now I would like to address other manifested forms of communication between us and our soul mates on the Other Side. These can be an almost infinite type and are hard to put into any one category, but I think the catch-all phrase for this type would be "visual messages".

Maybe a little background will help us to understand the process first – as much as can be understood anyway.

As we've already discussed, what we think of as the physical world – that which we can taste, touch, feel, hear, see – does not exist on the astral plane. Life there is made up of energy and thought – which is also energy. And energy, as anyone who has gotten an electrical shock knows, can move things and cause things to happen.

So far, so good.

Now factor in that time is a construct of this world as well and has no bearing on the dimension that our loved ones exist in and you have opportunities for some fantastic ways for our soul mates to get messages to us. So, let's explore some of those ways.

ELECTRICAL LIGHTS

One of the most commonly reported communications between loved ones on this side and the Other Side is through lights – flashing, buzzing, turning on and off in a rhythm. I cannot claim to know how they do this. All I know is that it is probably one of the most reported phenomena.

I can give you two specific examples from my own life with John.

When I walked into the kitchen on my first night home after John passed, one of the first things I noticed was that the overhead fluorescents lights were buzzing and flickering. We had lived in that house for many years and never had a problem with them. Occasionally the bulbs themselves would blow out and need to be replaced but this was different. Changing the bulbs didn't help. I tried that. I replaced the bulbs. I wiggled them in their sockets. Nothing helped. Eventually I gave in and just had the entire lighting system in the kitchen changed.

Another time about two months after John died, I was talking with my aunt on the phone in my living room. We were reminiscing about John and Aunt Mary was talking about our last day together with him and how good it had been. She then went on to say how much she missed John, how much she loved him, and how she still couldn't believe he was gone. Of course, I was saying the same things to her. Then as we were talking about all of this, the floor lamp across from me which was on up until that point, just simply blinked off. After a couple of seconds, while I watched it, it blinked back on again and remained fine for the rest of the day. I am sure John was acknowledging our conversation and trying to tell us that he was there and knew what we were saying. And maybe he was even saying how he thought our last days together had been nice too.

SONGS

Music has often been referred to as a universal language and with good reason.

Think about it. If you were watching a foreign film without subtitles, for instance, you would most likely have trouble understanding what was going on in any specific scene. Your only cues would be facial expressions and the music. Some facial expressions are also universal – smiling, laughing, tears, and expressions of fear and horror are all things we know instantly just by seeing them. But even those cues are denied to a blind person watching that film.

However, the chords of the music could still convey the emotion of that interaction between the characters to someone who could hear. And even some people with hearing difficulties report that they can "feel" the music by its beat and rhythm.

So, then it's no wonder music is so prevalent in all cultures and is forefront in their ceremonies.

I can be brought to tears by a beautiful piece played on a violin. Or swept away in emotion when I hear a stirring march. A song from our past can immediately bring us back to that time complete with the feelings.

Music reaches us in our core. Its energy is felt deep within us and moves our very soul.

Let's carry that thought further for a moment.

Music evokes emotion.

Emotion is energy.

At our essence, we are all energy.

Therefore, our loved ones who have passed who are still energy can manipulate energy to communicate with us.

Is it no wonder then that music is a very popular after-death communication device?

Let me give you a couple of examples that I have personally experienced.

One of my favorite movies of all time is "The Notebook". I

183

have a copy of the book and I watch that movie every time it's on television. I also own a copy of the movie just in case I have a sudden urge. Call me sappy but I'm a person who loves happily ever after no matter what.

And there's another more personal reason.

The story makes me think of John and me. I think Ryan Gosling even looks like John a little (especially with the beard). Maybe it's the strength and depth of the love of the two main characters. The feelings that movie evokes makes me sad but it makes me happy too. I am lucky to have had what I had with John and nothing can change that. I was (and am) loved by a wonderful, sweet, and special man.

So, one day a couple of years ago I downloaded the soundtrack to my Amazon music folder. But I did not sync my iPhone to it (this is important to remember). Then as luck would have it, the movie was on one of the TV stations that week and of course I watched it again. The very next day, I got in my car to go shopping and without me doing anything, my iPhone hooked up to my car via Bluetooth and started playing "I'll Be Seeing You" by Billie Holiday from The Notebook album!

What makes this even more astonishing is that I did not start up the program, the song was NOT downloaded to the phone program yet, and the song that was playing was the THIRD selection on the album. It wasn't even the first song. That took some manipulation on the part of my Honey. But he got my attention. I just sat there and listened, tears running down my face, absorbing the message that he was sending – that we are and would be together again.

I already told you about the incident in the airport the day John passed where he "caused" the song "Lyin Eyes" to play. I was frazzled. My flight was cancelled and I was rushing to catch a substitute flight an entire terminal away after hurriedly checking my and John's suitcases. As I was running to catch the tram to take me to the other terminal what played over the airport loudspeaker? "Lyin' Eyes". What were the odds? During that horrible day, John was trying to make me smile.

Music is a way for us to keep in touch. It's a way for our soul mates to reach out to us and tell us they are still here; we are still loved.

LICENSE PLATES AND REPEATED NUMBERS

Another method of communication might be a little harder to understand. I would not have believed it if I hadn't seen it with my own eyes. Not only is this possible but it is also very effective. Again, our loved ones take advantage of their non-time, non-linear dimension and the fact that they can send us thought messages that cause us to look at something at a specific time so that their message gets across.

John loves to send me messages via license plates. He knows that I pay attention to them. I have loved reading them since the craze of vanity plates has become so popular. It's fun to see what people like to put on the back of their car. John has said Hello to me more times than I can remember in this way but here is just one example. There is another in the last chapter that I will save until then.

Back in 2012, after John's mother passed away, I had to fly from Phoenix to Dallas, Texas and then drive (all by myself) from Dallas to Denison Texas for her memorial service and burial. I don't travel well when I am alone and I was especially worried about the drive. But John showed up. Not only did the song *Saturday Night Fever* play in the Dallas airport while I was getting my things together (a favorite song of ours) but as I was driving to Denison a car pulled in front of me and JOHN was on the license plate. I knew then everything would be okay and it was.

Numbers are another popular form of communication. Many people put stock in seeing repeated numbers such as 333 and 555. Of course, we can't prove that one way or the other but my philosophy is if it resonates for you and bears out, who am I to disagree? My personal focus is on a different set of numbers,

Joy Collins

however. John's birthday was April 13, 1943 or 4:13:43. He likes to use combinations of those numbers to get my attention.

A strong example happened just recently.

My goldendoodle Bella goes to daycare here in town. This one Saturday I was walking her back to the car when I saw a young gentleman getting out of his truck in the daycare parking lot. I knew we would have to pass him on the way to my car. Bella doesn't do well with strangers when she is with me. She immediately goes into protective mode. I prepared myself, holding her leash tightly and talking softly to her to try to get her to pass him without incident. It didn't work. Just as we passed the young man she started barking and lunging for him. I held on to her leash ever more tightly to control her. When she once again lunged, she pulled me down. I hit the pavement - hard, hitting my left knee. I still held on because I didn't want her to get away from me and I certainly didn't want her to hurt anyone.

By this time, the man was upset to see me fall and he leaned toward me to see if he could help and if I was all right. This upset Bella even more and she pulled on the leash again. This pulled me even further and I now hit the ground with my right hip and shoulder. At first, I thought I had broken my knee - I was nauseous from the pain. I must have been a sight lying there, dog barking, sunglasses askew. Despite the pain I could stand and gain control of Bella. I told the young man I was all right and hobbled to my car. I just wanted to get home. I got Bella into the back of my SUV and sat in the driver's seat, slowly breathing and trying to calm myself down. I was still nauseas and now everything was starting to hurt – a lot.

But I could move everything, so I drove home. Luckily, I only live about five minutes away from the day care center. On the way, I prayed. I was so afraid I was going to either pass out or throw up. "Please God, just get me home. John, if you're there, please be with me. I need help."

And that's when I saw it. I looked over at the digital clock on my dashboard computer and it said 4:43 - John's birthday month

186

and year. It made me feel so much better - I knew he was there. I knew I would be all right.

Not all of John's clock Hello's are this dramatic. Sometimes I will just be thinking about him and look at a clock and it will either be 4:13 or 4:43. Sometimes, they are associated with an event like the one I just relayed.

Or they can just be associated with an everyday occurrence that is meaningful to the two of us. For example, John used to always tease me about my love for Starbucks. Almost every time I went out shopping I would walk back in the house sipping a latte or something equally yummy. On one day, recently, I went into our local Starbucks for my usual and the computer wouldn't cooperate so the barista just gave it to me for free. When I got back to my car the computer clock read 4:43. John was still teasing me about my love of Starbucks.

OTHER ENERGY MANIFESTATIONS

This last category is a catch-all of things I just don't know where else to put.

People often report birds and insects as communications from their loved ones who have passed. Are our loved ones inhabiting those life forms? Of course not. But they can influence them to arrive at just the right moment to get our attention, make us think of them, and help us to know they are okay, they are here with us, and they love us.

So, a cardinal appearing on your lawn just as you feel yourself missing and loving your soul mate could be a sign that he/she knows what you are thinking and still loves you too. The same can be said of almost any animal or insect that either meant something to you and your love or gets you to notice something special that is part of a message. For instance, remember that dragonfly that practically rammed himself into my car door and then buzzed me again? He was obviously sent to get me to stop in my tracks and be watchful. The message was contained in the feather in

my path which I might not have ever seen otherwise.

Unusual lights might be another sign. Sometimes orbs on photographs are just tricks of light or moisture. But I have seen orbs in photographs that show up in only one photo while not being visible in another picture taken at the same time of the very same subject with the same camera. Sometimes they are not orbs at all but streaks of light. Again, all of this is energy manipulation to get our attention.

I had a profound experience a couple of years ago that I want to share. This occurred on a Sunday, in October of 2014. That morning, I had read an article about spirit communication. The article instructed the reader to ask for a sign from their loved one and then to be patient and wait to see what showed up. The final rule was to thank our loved after the sign was given.

So, I carefully followed the instructions. That morning I asked John for a sign, not requiring that it be anything specific, just something that would let me know it was him. Within a short period of time, there was a monarch butterfly in the back yard and then a little later the same butterfly flew outside my office window on the opposite side of the house. Then I started noticing number combinations occurring – 413, 443, 444, 555.

But the grand finale was a wonderful shaft of light. As I was leaving for Church that afternoon, I was idling in my car in the driveway while I set the security system. It's my habit to run through all the security cameras after I do that to make sure all is well and to check on my furbabies one last time before I leave. I have three cameras focused on various places inside the house and two outdoor cameras – one over the front door and one focused on the back deck, the deck that John built for us.

Imagine my shock, surprise, and wonder when I saw the feed from the deck camera! The light streaming down onto the deck resembled the shape of a tall man. Was it John? No, I don't believe the light was him per se. No, what I feel in my heart is that John could manipulate the light in a way that made it look like a person (him) and he inspired me to look at that camera just at the right moment. Regardless of how it worked, it was a beautiful communication and I thanked him for that big Hello (see this wonderful photo at the end of the book).

.

CONCLUSION

Does transitioning automatically turn our loved ones into some kind of quantum magician able to move things and bend light? Probably not. It does give them a different perspective and the properties of their world enables them to interact with our world in such a way that they can communicate with us in ways they couldn't before.

Regardless of how this all works, my point is that we should educate ourselves in the new ways that are now open to us so that our relationship can continue.

And always thank your loved one – preferably out loud – when they send you a wonderful Hello.

Chapter Twenty-Four

CB

This last chapter on ways to communicate with our soul mates who have passed is a little more esoteric, for lack of a better word.

I want to talk about meditation and just plain listening.

Meditation has become quite popular in the last couple of decades. People like Deepak Chopra and Wayne Dyer, and Neale Donald Walsch, to name just a few people, have made the practice mainstream. It's become fashionable which may or may not be a good thing. It's good because now it has lost its mystery (and people no longer consider it a strange Eastern practice) and bad because now everyone thinks it's easy and a quick (read "no work involved") way to achieve inner peace.

Meditation, like any other worthwhile practice, takes work and dedication. It is more than just sitting in one spot in yoga position for fifteen minutes to an hour and chanting "Om" and then automatically achieving nirvana. There are hundreds if not

Joy Collins

thousands of books and CD's out there, all promising to teach you the fine art of tuning into your inner self. I certainly cannot teach anything similar in a few paragraphs. I urge you to grab any of those fine books, etc., and start your practice.

What I will tell you, however, is that you must keep at it. It is easy to get discouraged and feel that you are not getting anything out of it and give up.

Please don't do that.

In addition to finding more peace and less stress in your life, meditation will have another benefit for those of us who are mourning our soul mate and yearning for communication.

Meditation will help to make that communication easier.

How?

I'm glad you asked.

Studies have shown that not only does meditation change your brain but the longer (i.e., more often over time) you meditate the more these changes expand exponentially. Some of these changes might be more easily noticeable. Those of us who meditate on a regular basis report feeling calmer, more centered, less likely to let things get to us on a large scale. In other words, we can let things slide off our back more easily.

I admit it's not easy and I still have my days where I want to punch walls but it's getting better.

But there are other, less noticeable changes that happen within the brain itself. The physical part of the brain called the pre-frontal cortex appears to change. This means that our thinking is affected for the better. Another part of our brain that controls emotions and fear is altered – the result is a more-modulated response to things that get our goat, so to speak.

And there is another more metaphysical response. Once we find ourselves more in tune with ourselves and our emotions, we also start to become more in tune with all things spiritual as well. Meditation helps our mind to become quieter and more open to our Higher Power and Higher Self. This in time helps us to become aware of that which is outside ourselves and realize that in fact,

192

Spirit is *inside* of us all the time. While this might sound circular, it's not. And finally, once we become more aligned with Spirit, our loved ones are now able to use that channel to communicate with us.

But this takes work. It takes practice. Daily practice.

I personally found this hard to do at first. My mind rebelled at being "quiet". As soon as I set aside time to what I envisioned "meditating" was, all kinds of thoughts started running around my brain.

Shopping lists.

To do lists.

Worrying.

Ruminating.

Worrying if I was meditating correctly.

Where was that blue sphere I was supposed to see?

Why isn't this WORKING?

Maybe you have been there too.

I knew I needed another way. So back to "lecture on Heaven" mode. I researched.

Books.

Tapes.

CD's.

And now in this digital age, MP3's.

I find I do better, at least at first, with guided meditations. There are hundreds, if not thousands, out there. Experiment. Find what works for you.

But the important thing is to do it. Set aside time every day to meditate, even if it is only for fifteen minutes. There are even walking meditation audios you can download that you can play on your phone while you just take a meaningful morning walk. That was how I got started. Just do whatever you need to do to get started.

I graduated from the morning walk meditation to then actually sitting (or lying down) every morning with a guided meditation on my iPhone. Now I alternate with those guided meditations and ones where I just sit in silence while the audio times me. I have found that my day goes much better when I start out with this time that I set aside for my Inner Self every day and the days that I don't do it, for whatever reason, I find that I miss it. It has now become my morning "fix" as it were. I feel better when I meditate so I keep meditating. And because I keep meditating, I feel better. So, I continue. And so on and so on.

But the best benefit of all is that now I feel more in tune with John. It is there on the astral plane that I can glimpse through mediation that he resides. It is there that he and I can communicate.

Do I hear conversations?

No.

Meditating has not produced a metaphysical telephone but my thoughts and his thoughts do sometimes align in a way that is pure mystery to me but wonderful, nevertheless. I can "feel" him for lack of a better word. And he can reach me in ways I never thought possible before. Remember we talked about extreme grief impeding signs for our loved ones? Well, a busy mind that is darting from thought to thought, worry to worry, can also inhibit communication from Spirit and our loved ones.

So, now, when I carry on a conversation with John in my head, if I quiet my mind, I am able to ascertain on occasion a thought that I feel does not originate with me and I have to assume might be coming from him.

I can best explain this with an example.

About three years ago the corner edge tile came off the bathroom vanity in the hallway bathroom. John had remodeled both bathrooms in our home and this was one of the tiles he had laid. I had no idea how to repair it but it needed to be put back on. So, I trotted myself down to the local hardware store here in town and asked one of the workers there. He guided me to glue that he swore would do the job.

It didn't.

As soon as it dried and I wiggled it, the tile came right back off in my hand.

I was frustrated and upset.

I remember walking into the living room and sitting on the

194

sofa and talking to John in my mind. I told him how sorry I was that I had ruined his hard work and how I needed to know how to fix it. I asked him to help me. And I trusted that he would.

At that point I just felt the need to go into the laundry room. Mind you, this was not some sort of huge revelation. There were no strange lights floating around the room. No apparitions or sounds. It was just a thought I had. So, I got up and walked into the laundry room. Then I just "felt" that I should look up. I did and I immediately saw on a shelf above me a large clear plastic lidded storage container that had beige colored stuff in it. I had no idea what it was but I grabbed a stepstool and climbed up to retrieve it.

Imagine my surprise when I took the container down and there in magic marker on the lid in John's handwriting were the words "tile adhesive". I couldn't believe it. He had truly helped me.

I opened the container, got a spatula from the garage, smeared that goop on the back of the guilty tile and smushed it back in place. That tile is still there to this day.

Was John communicating with me? I believe so. I had no idea the tile adhesive was there. I certainly didn't put it there. Obviously, John had put the leftover adhesive there after he remodeled the bathroom. He knew it was there.

How did this work? I can't say for sure. But my feeling is I leave myself open to communication, I practice that opening with meditation and calmness, and I trust in Spirit to help.

The topic of meditation and listening to the workings of Spirit can take up volumes in and of itself. If you are serious about communicating with your soul mate after death I highly recommend that you learn all you can about meditation and make it part of your daily routine.

There are other forms of communication such as using a pendulum and channeled writing, et cetera, but I am not proficient or knowledgeable enough to talk about those. My thinking is once you get started down this path, Spirit will guide you to what works for you. Be open to learning and a whole new world will appear before you.

Joy Collins

I also don't feel qualified to write an Appendix of suggested authors. Any trip to a bookstore or web site will show you that the options cannot be counted.

But I will list here a brief tally of the those who have influenced me the most. Often, these same authors will list an Appendix of their own. That is what happened to me – one author led me to another which led me to another and so on and so on.

In no specific order, I have enjoyed books and writings by the following:

MEDIUMS

James Van Praagh
John Holland
Allison DuBois
George Anderson
Suzanne Giesemann
Susanne Wilson
Mollie Morningstar
Jamie Clark

GRIEF

Tom Zuba
Joan Didion
John Chuchman, MA
C. S. Lewis

METAPHYSICAL TOPICS

Neale Donald Walsch
Deepak Chopra
Wayne Dyer
Mark Ireland
Michael Newton

Gregg Braden
Lynne McTaggart
James Redfield

AFTERLIFE/AFTERLIFE COMMUNICATION

R. Craig Hogan, PhD
Victor Zammit, JD
Bill Guggenheim
Rochelle Wright, MS
Marie Pe, Esq.
P.M.H. Atwater
Raymond Moody
Pim van Lommel, MD

REINCARNATION

Brian Weiss
Dick Sutphen
Robert Schwartz

This is a small list but will get you started. And keep in mind that not everything will resonate with you at first. I found the topic of investigating life in between lives to be almost preposterous at first but once I had a better understanding of things under my belt, that topic was a lot easier to understand. So much so that I was ready to explore my own life in between lives during that past life regression.

Chapter Twenty-Five

CB

This chapter is about the gifts of grief. And while that may seem like an impossible thing, just bear with me for a bit and I will show you what I mean.

I know where you are coming from. I can hear you yelling at me – "How can grief hold any gifts? This is the most horrible thing I have ever had to endure."

I would have said these very same things myself just a few years ago. But I have come to believe differently now. And while finding gifts inside this most dreadful of experiences might not seem like a way to communicate with our loved ones – and that is what I promised you at the beginning of this book – that too will come to light, I hope.

Let me try to explain. I've always been a planner. Anyone who knows me knows I have perfected planning to a fault. And I haven't met a spreadsheet I didn't like. I have always been a person who looked forward. Sometimes with anticipation, sometimes with dread. For me, there has always been the next challenge, the next event, the next fun thing to do with my Sweetheart. But I always struggled to be someone who lives in the Now, as the great sages tell us. I read about it. I meditated on it. It was something I knew I needed to work on. But its possibility always eluded me.

And then, when John transitioned, the days seemed to slide into each other. You might have felt that way, too. There were days I felt adrift. Without an anchor. Nothing to look forward to. Nothing had any meaning. John's passing had dropped me suddenly into foreign territory without a map, without knowing the language. It had thrown me off my axis.

I have already mentioned that John always told me things happen just the way they are supposed to. It's still hard for me to believe that some days. But I am learning that he was right. I am learning that even in my sorrow there are many gifts for me; blessings that I can find that I can hold on to. So, instead of looking forward to a future that seems empty to me, I am learning to look around me in the Now and appreciate what I find.

Let me explain further.

Over the course of our relationship and marriage, John and I enjoyed many different employment opportunities. As I've already mentioned, John started his professional career as a case manager/therapist in a child and adolescent mental health clinic. It was only after we married that he decided to go to nursing school. I have always been a nurse but I have worked in many different specialties - psychiatry mostly, but also preemie nursery, surgical, medical, operating room, just to name a few. Not only was I a bedside nurse but I worked my way through management from charge nurse of a shift to Head Nurse of a unit to Supervisor to eventually Director of Nursing. Later, I went back to school, got my degree and some additional training in legal nursing and forensics and started my own legal nurse consulting business. I think I enjoyed that the most.

But probably our most challenging professional episode was when John and I worked as nurses directly contracted by an agency

200

back in the late 80's to mid-90's. We were sent to places we would never have been otherwise. Because we could pick and choose where and when we worked, we chose to go to hospitals that really needed us and we picked shifts that paid the most. Often, this meant driving far from home to get to our assignment. Consequently, our most lucrative job was in Hershey Pennsylvania on the hematology/oncology unit. There we worked two sixteen-hour shifts every weekend, driving two and a half hours down from our home outside Wilkes Barre Pennsylvania on Friday afternoon and driving back home on Sunday morning. The upside to this grueling schedule was that we were off from Sunday to Thursday every week!

We had plenty of time to play and do other things and we were making what we liked to refer to as a "boatload" (at the time) of money. We were finally able to put money aside for retirement. But we could enjoy our time together too.

We took a vacation every month.

We slept in. We relaxed.

We were remodeling our home and had the time to do it.

And we had time to just enjoy each other's company.

John said over and over that were going to look back and call those days the "good old days". Except he said it in present tense at the time. "These *are* the good old days." I remember how much that impressed me at the time.

He was right, of course (although now I refer to all my days with John as the good old days).

But what he taught me was precious. He was telling me we needed to enjoy those days for what they were when they were, not wait until years down the road and then pine for them.

It was a valuable lesson.

One of the things I remember about my father is that he used to always say "Some day".

Some day we would...

Some day we would have...

Some day we would go...

201

Most of the time he never got to do or have any of those things and he missed what was in front of him along the way.

He was the opposite of the "good old days" theory. He was wishing for what hadn't happened yet.

That's not a good way to live either.

And I was in danger of carrying on that legacy until John.

John opened my eyes and my heart and for that I am very grateful.

Every day is a good old day.

Even if it's swinging on the porch swing with your honey.

Or sitting quietly and watching a bird hopping across the lawn.

Or looking at a sunset and admiring the beautiful colors.

Life is to be lived, not wished or pined for. Even this life that is filled with grief. It is here. Now. Not to be wasted.

Grief can leave you raw. Your feelings are suddenly very close to the surface. Since John died, I found that I cried more easily. Even in front of people. Which was new for me. But I also found that I felt my feelings more easily too and I still do to this day. And that can be a good thing. I am not as walled off as I was before. Before, John was the only person I opened up to. Now, because he is not here, I find myself willing to let others be there for me.

John is not physically here with me now but I can still look at the world as if he is. And I can be grateful for that gift he gave me and know it was given with love. When I stop and try to do that, I have been pleasantly surprised at what I have found.

A butterfly.

A baby quail.

My silly dog.

A friend's hug.

A stranger's smile - I even return it now.

One of the things I noticed after John passed was that I no longer got wrapped up worrying about small stuff. I am learning to let go of the ridiculous and the silly. I am getting good at letting go of grudges and anger. It doesn't mean I don't feel that stuff but I am better at letting it go. I used to love that song "Let It Go" from the movie *Frozen*. I had it on my iPhone and I would blast it in the car and sing along. But now I see life in a new way. Letting things go still implies a judgment. You're disapproving of something and then deciding to let it go. That's good but I now choose to take it a step further so my new mantra is the old song by The Beatles "Let It Be." I recognize what bothers me but I don't make a judgment over it. I just acknowledge it and let it be. It's separate from me and I can move away from it. In the end, it doesn't matter, and I will not spend my energy on it. I'm not saying this is easy. It takes work. But the result is so freeing. I imagine this is how our loved ones feel on the Other Side. They can see things from a perspective that we can't. But that doesn't mean that we can't try.

I forgive those who have "wronged" me (if, in fact, anyone can truly do that – in actuality, being wronged is our perception, not theirs). It doesn't mean that I allow them in my space any more. And it doesn't mean that what they did was all right. It just means I work at not dwelling on it and giving them free rent in my head. John was very good at this by the end of his life. So, his gift to me is to encourage me to strive for that peace of mind too.

I know he was ready when he left us. I want to be ready too.

I'm sure you have figured out from all my John stories that he loved to laugh. I was always the more serious one. But now, even though it feels hard to laugh, I still try. I know John wants me to. And I have found when I am open to laughter, I find it in the strangest places.

Case in point was when I decided it was time to find a place to store John's ashes and mine, when the time comes. We had never discussed that. Ever. I had gotten a very nice urn for John but that was as far as it went. About a year and half after John passed, I contacted a church a few towns over that had a columbarium (a room or building with niches for funeral urns to be stored - a new word for me), made an appointment to speak with a representative, and off I went. It was an experience, to say the least. I don't know if it was typical, but it was different. To start with, I was given a list of

Joy Collins

available spaces to choose from, each having a certain price allotted to them depending on location - higher on the wall was more expensive than lower, glass front cost more than closed, and so forth. I was having trouble maintaining my composure. I was starting to hear John laugh in my head.

Then I was offered a "tour" to see where the real estate was located. The lobby of the columbarium building had piped in music and a "visiting" room. My guide then proceeded to show me where various people she thought I might know (local well-known families) were going to be laid to rest as well as the space she and her friends had already purchased. It begged the question why I would have to know this. Surely, we were not going to all party after lights out. But I smiled and nodded my way through the walk-through. John was now laughing out loud.

Finally, we went back to her office and she presented me with a price sheet and finance plan, expecting me to make a choice, implying if I waited too long, the choice spots would be gone. I felt like I was in a time-share presentation. I excused myself to go to the ladies' room. While in there I could swear I heard John yelling "Get out!" in between absolute belly laughs. I went back in, told the nice lady I needed time to think and quickly left. She called a week later and I let her go to voice mail. John is still in his urn and I still have no pre-plans made. And every time I decide it's time to try again, John just keeps laughing. And every time I remember that incident, I laugh, too. And I thank John for that gift.

Perhaps, most importantly, I have been given the gift of gratitude. Gratitude for the life John and I shared, and the love we were blessed with. Gratitude for the gift of a mate so perfect that I felt almost perfect too. No, he was not a perfect person. None of us are. But he was perfect for me. I could not have become the person I am now had it not been for him.

And finally, I have been given the gift of fearlessness in the face of death. I welcome it now and that has freed me to see life in a much different way.

I am going to pay this gift forward. It gives me pleasure to do so because I am spreading love instead of fear and it makes me feel good to do it in John's name, keeping his spirit alive on this Earth.

And, in that way, as I promised John on the day he died, we are doing this together. We are still connected. This is still our marriage.

We are still One.

Soul mates.

Twin Flames.

Together.

Photographs

_cs_

On the following pages are some of my favorite photos of John, John and me, and some of the signs he has sent me since his death.

Baby John

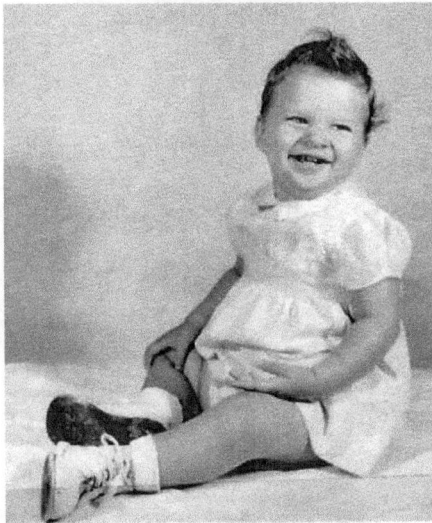

Baby Joy

Joy Collins

John in the Air Force, 19 or 20 years old, around 1963

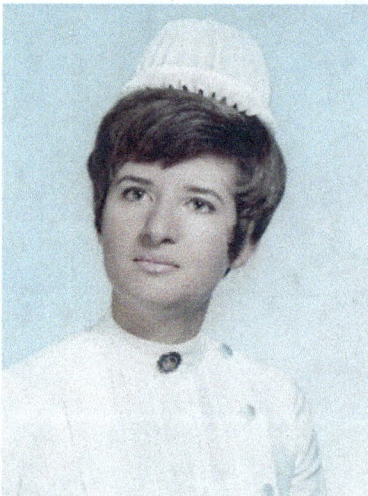

Me, Graduation from Bellevue Nursing School, 1968

Our wedding day, August 28, 1981

One of my very favorite photos. This was our first dance at our reception after our Church wedding March 19, 1988

John with our two dogs – Jessie and Toby

The house in Lehman after its loving restoration

On a cruise 2005

John and I on our last weekend together May 21, 2010

I was having breakfast alone at Sofrita's, a restaurant in Fountain Hills, the week of our anniversaries in March 2012 (we always celebrated March 15, 17 and 19 as days that were special to us) and was feeling sad because John wasn't with me. The waitress brought my cappuccino that I had ordered. She said she had ordered one too and the chef had made this for her, but she wanted me to have it and she would get another. I know the hearts were from John.

On March 17 of that same year I met a friend for breakfast. She gave me a belated birthday present (my birthday was March 1st – my second without John). The little statue is making the sign for "I Love You."

Roses for my birthday from Linda (and John) March 2013. Linda met me for High Tea at the Ritz-Carlton in Phoenix. She told me she just "felt" that she needed to bring me these roses.

Joy Collins

On March 1, 2014 (another birthday), I told John I would love a sign from him so that I would know he was with me that day. I told him I would love it if somehow he could send me roses and it would be extra special if they were not red. Then I met some friends for tea in Phoenix. I thought maybe my roses would arrive at tea. Maybe my friends would bring me flowers – like the year before. Or maybe the Ritz would have roses on the table. But none of that happened. I was a little disappointed but I thought I had been asking a lot anyway and I should not be so greedy. The day was wonderful and I was happy to be with my friends.

So, I came home. Then I heard the mail being delivered. As soon as the mail truck pulled away, I went out the front door to go to the mailbox. As I was closing the screen door, I felt something under my hand. I looked down and on the doorknob was a notice from a local florist to go next door to pick up some flowers that had been delivered and left there for me. Off I went. Imagine my surprise and utter joy when I saw these flowers waiting for me - and the roses are peach and a deep pink! They were sent to me by my cousin, engineered I am sure by my sweet, sweet Love.

I took this picture when I wasn't feeling well at all, right before I was diagnosed with Valley Fever. It's not an orb but this is the only picture this shape (upper right corner) appeared in. I took a series of photos with the same camera in the same light and this shape does not appear in any of the others. This is over the spot where John and I always sat together in the morning having coffee and chatting before we started our day.

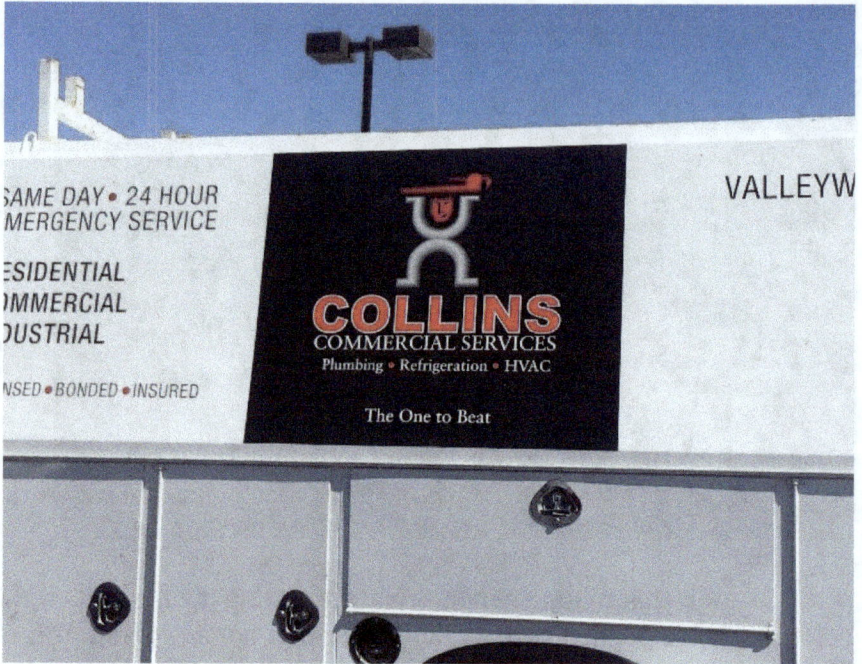

I pulled into the parking lot at Costco one day and saw a spot I wanted. But a gentleman was loading his purchases into his car and his door was protruding into the space, so I moved on. And then I spied another spot I thought would be good. As I neared it I knew it was the spot meant for me and John was also saying Hello. Parked next to the open parking spot was this truck and this was on its side.

March 1, 2015

I wanted roses for my birthday again, but I felt that ordering them myself was cheating so I didn't. Then the morning of my birthday there was an email from FTD reminding me that "Today is Joy's birthday" and did I want to send flowers to her?

I figured - what the heck - it couldn't hurt to look. So, I logged into my FTD account and started browsing. Sure enough, there was an option to send flowers for delivery that very day. I made a search and asked it for the lowest priced flowers - just to see. No point in being crazy about this. Lo and behold - a single rose popped up.

I remembered how John used to bring me a single red rose every Friday and then monthly on our first date anniversary. I thought that was a hint from him, so I clicked on it. It was reasonable and came in its own vase. I was going to get the single rose and then decided to upgrade the order and get two roses, signifying the two of us. I placed the order.

This is what arrived. John sent me three roses!

I know I paid for two. I checked the order and the receipt that came with the flowers verified it.

But there are clearly three roses here. So, I guess I have the two I ordered, and the one John wanted to send.

Joy Collins

The day after Christmas 2015 I found this heart-shaped little piece of paper in my bed. I think the cat left it there with a little "help."

The feather that John sent to me after the "bump in the night"

John's picture in a frame with his stone angel message attached.

October 12, 2014
This is the light that showed up on the security camera the day I asked John for a sign.

Chapter Twenty-Six

 C3

And so, we come to the end of this book.

But not to the end of any of our stories.

I hope I have given you hope. And that I have encouraged you.

Communication with your loved one, your soul mate, is possible. I can honestly attest to that. And it seems to me that the more in tune I get with John, the more we can communicate. I can only imagine how it must be for our loved ones on the Other Side. How frustrating sometimes to want to be able to get a message to us and not have us able to receive it. Maybe like the old days of the rabbit ears on TV's when all you got was fuzz no matter how much aluminum foil you attached to the ends of the antennae. But now, if we practice perceiving the signs, we get a better TV antenna system and a better signal.

Maybe that's a poor analogy but I think you get my point.

I know in my heart that the signs I receive are real. They

must be. One might be a fluke. Two might be a coincidence. Three might be wishful thinking. But this has been happening repeatedly. I have to trust. John is here with me and he wants me to know that. The stories I have written in this book are only a small sampling of what I have experienced in the last few years. I have tried to pick the ones that I thought would best exemplify what I have been trying to say.

Perhaps this last story will help the most.

Recently I was driving to meet some friends. The event was a play and while I knew Cathy, the person who invited me to join the group, I didn't know any of the other women. There were going to be six of them that were strangers to me, a situation I found unnerving. My therapist had been working with me to get out into the world more and enjoy new experiences. When I hesitated, and referred back to how much easier this was when John was here, her response was to take him with me, to ask him to accompany me. So, on this occasion, I reluctantly agreed. Yet, despite that promise, I almost cancelled several times. But in the end, I decided to go. I think it was more that I didn't want to have to report back in my next session that I had chickened out.

So, as I drove to meet Cathy, I spoke to John. "Please be with me, Baby. You know how I am in new situations. I wish you were with me but if you could just accompany me in my heart that would be great."

While I was driving, I was also playing my new Josh Groban album on my iPhone, pumping it via the Bluetooth through my car speakers. Right after I said my little prayer to John one of my all-time favorite songs came on "You'll Never Walk Alone." Josh did a great job with it and I was carried away by the emotion of the song. Just then a white SUV pulled up next to me on my left and then sped up a little way so that I could now see its license plate. Imagine my surprise to see "JONNY" in large letters. Mind you, "You'll Never Walk Alone" was still playing loudly in my car.

The car stayed with me for that song and the next one and then pulled to my right and exited to another street and was gone.

But the message was received. John was with me. I smiled and said Thank you.

But it doesn't end there.

The following week I was again driving. This time I was on my way to pick up Bella from day care. Again, I was playing Josh's album and once again had come to that song. I was enjoying it and remembering what had happened the last time I had heard it. I was feeling thankful for the message from John.

And then it hit me. Not only had John been telling me he would be with me that particular day, but he was telling me that he would *always* be with me. That was the real message. I am not alone, and I won't be as long as I am alive on this planet. John loves me with all his heart. That won't change just because we are separated by different dimensions.

And that is the message for all of us. Our loved ones are with us. If we have been lucky enough to have been mated to our soul mates/twin flames, our loved ones are with us in ways we cannot even imagine. We must but stop and think and remember and we can feel their love surrounding us. They will always be there for us. No, it's not the same. Of course, it's not. But we are still here for a reason. Our time will come when it's supposed to.

In the meantime, we are not alone.

That's when I knew. That was John's message for me and what he wants my message to be for you. So, I decided that that is the title for my book, this book. I had been struggling with finding one I liked up until then, trying out different titles but none seemed to work.

Now I knew in my heart what it was, and it felt right.

Just as John had told me years before on the little stone angel:

I will never leave you...

Joy Collins trained as a nurse at well-known Bellevue Hospital in New York City and then went on to receive her BS in Business Administration from St. Joseph's College. In addition, she studied Reiki with Susanne Wilson, a medium and Reiki Master in Carefree, Arizona and is now a Reiki Master herself.

She started her writing career penning non-fiction articles. Then came two contemporary novels in the women's fiction genre – *Second Chance* and *Coming Together* (co-authored with Joyce Norman).

Joy's life took an unexpected turn when her husband John died suddenly in May 2010. In trying to make sense of that loss, she combined her love of writing and her passion for all things spiritual with her love for her beloved husband. *I Will Never Leave You* is the result of that endeavor. It is her passion to help those who have lost their soul mate to death.

A transplanted Easterner, Joy now calls Arizona home. In her spare time, Joy enjoys mothering her four furbabies - energetic goldendoodle Bella and marmalade kitties Riley, Chaz, and Sean. Follow her at www.joycollins.com .

www.ingramcontent.com/pod-product-compliance
Lightning Source LLC
LaVergne TN
LVHW021133080426
835509LV00010B/1333